AUDITION ARSENAL FOR MEN IN THEIR 30s

101 Monologues by Type,
2 Minutes & Under

A Smith and Kraus Book
Published by Smith and Kraus, Inc.
177 Lyme Road, Hanover, NH 03755
www.smithandkraus.com

First Edition: August 2005
10 9 8 7 6 5 4 3 2 1

Manufactured in the United States of America
Interior Text Design by Julia Gignoux, Freedom Hill Design
Cover Design by Alex Karan of Blaise Graphics, www.blaisegraphics.com

The Library of Congress Cataloging-In-Publication Data
Audition arsenal for men in their 30s : 101 monologues by type, 2 minutes
& under / edited by Janet B. Milstein. —1st ed.
p. cm. — (Monologue audition series)
Includes bibliographical references.
ISBN 1-57525-399-2
1. Monologues. 2. Acting—Auditions. I. Milstein, Janet B. II. Series.

PN2080.A75 2005
813'.045089286—dc22
2005044122

AUDITION ARSENAL
FOR MEN IN THEIR 30s

101 Monologues by Type, 2 Minutes & Under

EDITED BY JANET B. MILSTEIN

MONOLOGUE AUDITION SERIES

A Smith and Kraus Book

Acknowledgments

I would like to express my deepest gratitude to
Eric Kraus and Marisa Smith for entrusting me with this project
and for their wisdom, patience, and generosity.

I would also like to thank the following people
for their help and support:

Karen Milstein
Barbara Lhota
The Milsteins
Alex Karan
Russ Tutterow
Sandy Shinner
Keith Huff
Karen Vesper
Tom Volo
Julia Gignoux
Susan Moore

All of the wonderful actors who took the time to give their input
and all of the talented writers who shared their work with me.

Contents

PERSUASIVE/INSPIRATIONAL

HAUNTED/GUILT-RIDDEN

ROMANTIC/IN LOVE

HIGH-STRUNG/NEUROTIC/STRESSED-OUT

Audition Arsenal Introduction

Redefining the monologue book

When Eric Kraus approached me about editing a new series of monologue books based on character type, some questions immediately came to mind: Was this type as in theater or film? Most specific types fall under film, yet monologues are rarely used for film or on-camera. For theater there are really only three main types: Leading Man/Lady, Ingénue/Young Man, and Character Actors. If I wanted to offer more detailed types, what criteria would be most useful? Would profession be considered a type? How about funny? Could social status define type?

In addition, I considered what was needed in a monologue book that had not yet been addressed. How would I improve upon the monologue books I own? What would make a book more valuable? How could I create a book to solve the problems my students are constantly voicing? As an actor, writer, and monologue coach, I wanted this new monologue series to give actors what they truly need for auditions. I had my own ideas about what *I* would find useful, but I decided to poll some actors to get their input, as well. The actors had a lot of common requests that confirmed my initial instincts. Most importantly this series would need to maximize the number of monologues an actor would actually use from one source. To do that, the traditional monologue book would need to be reinvented.

How are the books in this series better?

When I was studying acting in college, I'd always wished that there were monologue books just for actors in their twenties. And my dream books would have taken it a step further and been separated by gender to increase the number of monologues in one book that specifically applied to me. Now, I am presenting that to you — Women 20s, Men 20s, Women 30s, and Men 30s. No more skipping over pages and pages because the characters are out of your age range or not for your gender. Within each book, the choices are plentiful, and you're sure to find pieces that fit your specific needs.

That brings me to the next revolutionary feature of the Audition Arsenal series: The books are organized by type. By type, I'm referring to the most prominent quality the monologue reveals about the actor. So instead of being typed somewhat generically (eg, waitress or Ingénue), the monologues are designed to show you possess the qualities crucial to a particular character or role. Auditioning for a Harry Kondoleon play? Check out the High-strung/Neurotic/Stressed-out category. Want to get a callback for that Durang play? Prepare one of the Wacky/Quirky/Odd pieces.

Not only can you use these monologues to audition for a specific role, but you can use them to show your range in general auditions. When asked to prepare two contrasting pieces, you can go beyond simply a comedic and a dramatic (or a contemporary and a classical, if requested), and demonstrate significantly contrasting personas. Put yourself in the director's chair. Which would be more interesting to see an actor perform — a blunt, strong comedic piece with a blunt, strong dramatic piece or a vulnerable comedic piece with an intimidating/dangerous dramatic?

As actors, we must remember that directors are often meeting us for the first time and might assume that we can play only what we show them. So by all means show them! Think of the different impressions you make with your classmates versus coworkers, or on a first date versus a job interview. The pieces you choose tell directors something about you and your capabilities. Sell your strengths, cast yourself against your usual type, and prepare your personal "arsenal" of monologues so you'll be ready for any upcoming audition — no matter what it calls for.

Here are some additional bonuses you'll find in this series:

- The monologues are two minutes and under — some are one minute and under — to fit the time constraints of auditions.

- Very few, if any, of the monologues sound classical. Why? If you are required to do a classical and a contemporary monologue, you want them to contrast as much as possible.

- Only a small number of the monologues require dialects or accents. Why? The rule of thumb is to avoid dialect pieces in auditions unless they are specifically requested. If your accent is not dead-on directors tend to focus on the accent rather than the acting.

- There are 101 monologues to choose from in each book!

- The monologues are from plays as opposed to self-contained pieces. Some of the writers, kindly, at my request, edited the pieces slightly or pasted dialogue so that the monologues would be better suited to audition situations. However, when you read the play, you will see the bulk of the monologue in the same form and that the character and his or her situation have not changed.

- I have included a Tips section in each book containing helpful information that pertains to the selection and preparation of monologues.

I hope you find this new monologue series to be as valuable, time-saving, and innovative as I have set out to make it. In this particular book, I anticipate that you'll find a plethora of monologues to use for upcoming auditions. But don't let that stop you from checking out all of the books in the Audition Arsenal series. I wish you the best of luck in all of your endeavors. And when auditioning, have fun and break a leg!

Janet B. Milstein
www.janetmilstein.com

Tips for Selecting and Preparing a Monologue

Selection

Choose monologues that make you laugh, cry, feel, or think: "I can relate to this!" If a piece speaks to you, even it makes you angry, chances are you will naturally be invested in the piece.

Although each monologue in this book falls into your age range, you should still consider whether you could realistically be cast in this role. If not, choose another piece.

Find a piece that helps you shine. When reading a monologue ask yourself if it really shows what you can do or if it sells you short.

If you are selecting a monologue for a specific role in an upcoming audition, be sure the monologue reveals that you possess the crucial qualities needed to play that role.

If you are preparing for generals and are selecting two or more monologues, choose contrasting pieces that effectively demonstrate your range.

The monologues in this book are two minutes and under. However, you may have auditions that ask for two monologues to be performed in three minutes, or for one-minute monologues. When choosing pieces, make sure they fit the requirements. It is not professional to run overtime. In some cases you may even be timed. Therefore, it is best to keep your monologue at least ten seconds shorter than the allotted time slot. Also, keep in mind when you are reading and timing your monologue(s) that performing time will run longer than reading time.

Pick your monologue(s) now! Don't put it off. Choosing a monologue that fits you well, reading the play, and working and memorizing the piece all take time. If you wait until the last minute, you will not be adequately prepared. Unlike cold readings, monologues give you the chance to show what you're capable of when you have time to prepare a piece.

Preparation

In terms of preparing a monologue for use in auditions, there is much work to be done. Depending on where you are in your process and which methods you are studying, you will work differently. However, I find the following steps to be useful regardless of the method you subscribe to and the extent of your acting experience.

Read the play your monologue is from in its entirety. It will help you to understand the character, history, relationship, setting — everything that is needed even when you only perform the monologue. Not only will it help you to clarify your choices and understand the circumstances, but you just might find a new role, play, or author to add to your list of favorites!

If you have difficulty locating the play, look in the permissions section in the back of the book to contact the author or the author's agent to obtain a copy. If that information becomes outdated, check with Smith and Kraus to see if they can help put you in touch with the right person.

Answer the questions below with respect to your monologue and write your answers in the first person (e.g.: I am twenty-eight, I want her to . . .).

Who are you talking to? Make it very specific, not just "a friend" or "Kate." Use the script for clues about your relationship and fill in the rest.

What is your objective (goal, intention, "fighting for")? It must include the other person. What do you want from him or her? Make it specific and bold — go for your dream goal!

When and where is this taking place? Be very specific as it will inform your environment, your body, and much more.

What happened the moment before the monologue begins? What did the other person say or do that compels you to speak the first line (and the rest of your monologue) right now — not two weeks ago, not yesterday, not an hour ago? The moment before is so important. Test it out and fine-tune it until you have chosen something big enough and personal enough to springboard you into the monologue.

Go through the text of your monologue and with a pencil divide the monologue into beats. Look for the major and minor transitions in the text and use your own system to mark them. Do not skip this step or your monologue will likely be on one note.

How are you going to accomplish your objective — achieve your goal? With tactics or actions. These are the things you do to get what you want. When choosing actions or tactics, put them in the form "to verb" the other person. For example: to beg her, to threaten him, to charm her. Go back to your text, think about your objective, and choose an action/tactic for each beat. Test it out, refine it. The text will help you choose. However, be careful not to be so rigid with this process that your monologue loses spontaneity. Over time, you should change your actions if they get stale.

Personalize your monologue. Are there past events, situations, or other characters mentioned in the text? This is one of the most enjoyable parts of the process — let your imagination run wild and fill in the details that are *not* given in the script (but fall under the given circumstances). Be creative and have fun, but don't stop until you create specifics that will live in you fully.

Memorize your monologue inside out and upside down. I recommend memorizing by rote — quickly and without emotion or expression so as not to get stuck in a line reading. The idea is to drill the lines so well that you never have to be *back in your head* thinking about them when you should be *out in front of you* fighting for your objective from the other person.

Work your monologues with a coach, teacher, director, or fellow actor. Auditioning can be intimidating and what we do when performing alone often changes in the presence of others. You cannot be truly focused on achieving your goal if you are trying to direct yourself at the same time. Work with someone who will be supportive yet honest. No matter where we are in our acting careers, we never stop growing and we all need other people to help guide us.

Acting is a shared experience between performers and audience — even when performing monologues. Remember, you may be auditioning by yourself, but you still have an audience and they're rooting for you.

Men-Oh-Pause
By Lauren D. Yee

Lucas: male, late twenties to late thirties; a typical guy with a private
  sensitive side

Comic

*Lucas speaks to his wife Ellen about his rare genetic disor-
der, which will eventually turn him into a woman.*

LUCAS: Ellen, I can't help it. You think I want to be a woman? It's a
genetic thing. It runs in the family. When my dad hit thirty, he
went from Frank to Franny — which upset a couple guys at the
country club. But my mom dealt with it fine! She grew to enjoy
it. *(Beat.)* Really. It's like Julie Andrews in *Victor/Victoria* — in
the end, who cares if she's a man or not? And we've always been
best friends, haven't we? And this will only make us closer.
Remember that time when you were throwing up in the women's
toilet because you ate that fish and messed up your shirt? Well,
next time you barf your brains out, I'll be able to go with you
and hold back your hair. Just like it should be. Now you won't
have to coordinate my outfits or tell me what to buy for your
birthday or complain about me leaving the toilet seat up.
(Notices Ellen continuing to watch TV.) Because Ellen — *(Begins
to insert himself between Ellen and TV.)* — Dr. Nick says we do
need to be *sensitive* at a time like this. *(More irked and builds
steadily until eruption.)* And *respect* one another. And hear what
each other has to say. Are you listening to me, Ellen? Because I
really don't think you can hear me with the game on. Honey, it's
a *commercial*. Look at me, Ellen. Look at me. I think it's about
time you stop blocking me out and for once — just once in your
goddamned, beer-stained, football-obsessed life — listen to *my*
needs! I'm your WIFE, God damn it, and I think it's about time
you realized that! *(Beat, pulls anger and frustration back in, tries
to end with dignity, icily.)* Because really, honey, it's not fair for
me. *(As a guilt trip.)* Or the children. *(Waits for Ellen's reaction,
there is none.)* I'll be in the kitchen. *(Stops, turns head back.)*
We're having casserole tonight.

4 Murders
By Brett Neveu

Mitch: twenty-five to thirty-five, a mid-level workaholic business-man

Seriocomic

> *Mitch is speaking to Joel, a man whom he perceives to be a food-delivery person. Previously alone in his office and rather anxious, Mitch coaxes Joel into conversation. He begins to ask Joel his opinion on various topics including employment, the nature of truth, and what reasons he feels exist that Mitch's tropical-flavored drink may have dyed his tongue red.*

MITCH: My tongue is red because of all the red dye that is put into tropical punch. It "temporarily" dyes the consumer's tongue red. How long, do you suppose, it takes for this red tongue to dissipate? Care to take a guess? It takes one full day. Why? They use very strong dye, something that could, if ingested in great quantities, could possibly kill you. But I am getting off-topic and now you'll think this information I've told you about the shockingly strong red dye in tropical punch drink is an untrue story when in fact it is true. This, I'm about to tell you, this is the untrue story. Listen to this falsehood: There are sounds in this building. Sounds without cause. A person, walking through this building, hears sounds. *(Pause.)* It isn't true. *(Pause.)* But if it were true, that odd sounds were happening, odd sounds emanating from a place that does not exist, that would be a bit disconcerting, don't you agree? *(Pause.)* It is true. There are sounds that are heard, by me, in this building, sounds created by no one, sounds that come from no place. And I hear those sounds, I hear them late at night, at times like these, late, the sounds such as "Zip!" and "Wahh!" Listen. Let's listen and see if we hear those sounds.

Billy and Dago
By Charles Evered

Dago: thirties, a vagabond and streetwise fellow

Comic

Dago recalls running into an old friend.

DAGO: Hey, have you heard what happened to Tommy Rifkin? He's colonial now. I am not kidding you. Tommy Rifkin! Goofball "under the tracks" Rifkin from Vreeland Ave. is colonial — like you know, Ben Franklin. And as this is my hand in front of me I'm walkin' down State Street not seein' anybody I know, when all the sudden Tommy pops outta some alley way ahead of me and I see he's wearin' all that colonial crap, you know, like stockings and a triangle hat and those stupid pilgrim shoes and crap. I was sure it was him because I remembered his geeky walk — and so I remember he owes me like fifty bucks that he blew on the track a few years ago. So I run up to him and I go; "Hey, Tommy." And I swear to God he turns to me and goes; "May I prithee help you, sir?" Or something like that. And I go "Tommy, it's me!" And he starts lookin' at me like I'm nuts and so I just start askin' 'im where he's livin' and stuff and he says somethin' like; "I hold my estate in the great Commonwealth of Virginia, sir." And I go; "Yeah? Where?" And he goes, "Williamsburg." And that's when it dawns on me. Tommy Rifkin *is* colonial. He's turned into one of those weird colonial people from Colonial Williamsburg. I'm telling you, it's like a cult down there. Once you start bein' colonial, you can't stop. It's like a form of brainwashing is what it is, really. Tommy Rifkin. Colonial. What is *that* about?

Neverland
By Jonathan Dorf

Peter: thirty-four, a homeless man who has finally hit rock bottom

Comic

> *Wendy, who is Peter's age and volunteering for an outreach program, is trying to give homeless Peter a tongue sandwich. He's doing his best to keep her at bay.*

PETER: I've infected you. *(Beat.)* It's *me.* It's always me. My mother hated me. *(Beat.)* I saw a man on the next block wearing a bra and going from can to can, sampling everybody's garbage. He didn't have a tongue. If he's not full, he might want those tongue sandwiches. I think his name is Bob. I think it's Bob because I called him Jesus once and he didn't answer. I have to go. The police come around at ten and chase everybody out. They'll hit you with a baton if you don't leave fast enough. I got a leg cramp once, so I couldn't get up as fast as they wanted me to. Thwack. Guy was late for watching pro wrestling at the bar around the corner. Thwack. Hurt like a bitch for a month. I'm thirty-four. My body feels like it's seventy-four. What time is it?
(Peter gathers his stuff, such as it is.)
Sometimes they come early.

FYI

By Barbara Lhota and Janet B. Milstein

Donald: thirties, the son of the CEO

Comic

Cheryl, twenties, has applied for a new position in a different section of her company. The director of this area, Donald, thirties, has called her in for an interview today. Cheryl has been incredibly nervous all morning. This is exactly the kind of promotion she wants. Donald, whose father owns the entire business, tends to act defensively when asking people about their qualifications because he is less than qualified. To make up for his lack of education and experience, he has made a habit of creating new work-related acronyms in an effort to confound his underlings.

DONALD: Save it. Marla has a copy. I prefer to look at people without seeing all their past education. I mean, who cares in the end? Who cares! So you got a masters from Brown. Just a bunch of letters. You don't think I have an education? You don't think I earned this? Just because my father owns this place, you think I just got a free ride? *(Cheryl shakes her head no furiously. Sighs. Shakes his head no.)* OK, I did, but that's not the point. Sure, you may know how to program this or that. Sure, you may know how to read three languages. But la-de-dah. Competence is overrated. Who said that's all I wanted? In the end, what matters is how *symbiotic* you are with us, right? Difficult questions must be answered. Will you be part of our team? Will you bring something to the table? Will you spontaneously bring in Crispy Creams? Just kidding. Now really. Will you be in harmony with our symphony or will you simply suck — in other words, O.O.T.N.? *(Nodding.)* Right? You see? *(Beat.)* This is what matters. O.O.T.N. Do you understand what I'm saying? Out-of-tune nincompoop, Cheryl. Out-of-tune nincompoop. I'll say it again. Out-of-tune nincompoop. *That's* what matters. *(Nodding.)* See? You can't get that from a resume. I want to see *you* — the *real* you, the undocumented you, the unrevised, unedited, unaltered, bare naked you!

Tapster
By N. M. Brewka

Phil: male in late twenties upwards

Comic

> *Phil, a transgendered bar owner who was once called Elizabeth-Grace, interviews Brian, straight, a fairly low achiever, and longtime college student.*

PHIL: Well, Brian, I'm really pleased to hear that your beverage of choice is tap water. I mean, really, it's such a blessing to know that even if you swill, the till will fill. Didn't know you'd be employed by a poet, did you? When I was at Smith — and believe you me, I was so misguided I was thrilled when the trustees absolutely refused to let a man in to do anything other than dig a ditch — I won three sonnet prizes. Of course, back in those days I was called Elizabeth-Grace. Yes, I insisted on the full moniker. I wasn't going to be any Betty Boop-boop-adoop, believe you me. You know, Brian, the funny thing is, when I had the change of life — yes, that's what I like to call it because after all, it was Adios, estrogen, wasn't it — I started talking like this and I can't for the life of me figure out why. Well, slide over, sugar, and I'll show you how to pull a tap so it comes out all creamy.

Black Now Blue
By Adam Simon

Herm Randazzik: an odd CEO in his late thirties

Seriocomic

Although he's the only one who knows it, Herm Randazzik is about to be in the center of a huge corporate scandal involving improper accounting practices that he ordered. In his yearly video message to the stockholders he loses control and finally comes clean. Herm has just arrived at the office, set his things down, taken a deep breath, and started recording on a video camera.

HERM: Well, stockholders as my time here draws to a close . . . there's a few things that . . . Um, I should just — I'm not very good at my job. I feel like I should go ahead and get that out of the way before we move on. And this isn't just me fishing for compliments or beating myself up or anything. I'm legitimately bad at it. The very fact that I was ever hired is a pretty troubling indication of where this company, this company that you have invested your money in, a decision that I would never make, well it says a lot about the company. I am, after all, in a position to lose you a significant amount of money. Which I have. And for that . . . sorry. *(Pause.)* I'm convinced that it only takes two things to make it as a CEO. If you wanna be a CEO listen up, it's easy really. First, it's good to have a really solid believable look of intense decision making. You know what I'm talking about. It looks kind of like this.
(He does a face of intense decision making and makes audible thinking noises.)
  You're probably thinking "I know that face." And if we've ever had a conversation then yeah, you do know that face. The moment someone walks into my office, it's like an instinctual reaction. Suddenly my face looks like I'm doing intense math equations in my head or contemplating the entire stock market. It doesn't matter what you ask, "Is my fly unzipped?" or "How can we simultaneously maintain market viability while keeping

and possibly giving a raise to our current workforce?" Either way, the response will look something like this: *(Intense decision-making face.)*

The second thing you need is a massive sense of entitlement because otherwise you'll do what I'm doing today. You'll realize that you don't deserve what you've got. And once you're here it's hard to go anywhere else at that point. At least upward. I mean you can retire. And that's what I'm doing. So in closing, sell your stocks. Today. Seriously. I can't stress this point enough.

Spare Somethin'?
By Barbara Lhota and Janet B. Milstein

Sammy: thirties, a drunk who always has a story to get some spare change

Comic

When Sammy spots the well-dressed Lorna heading toward the train station, he grasps the opportunity to hit her up for some money. Unfortunately, Sammy is in for a lot more than he bargains for when he realizes that Lorna is a mental patient at the nearby Rock Creek Facility.

SAMMY: You're crazy. You are one crazy bird. You look all dressed up, like you're steppin' out of a Christian Du Jour Catalogue, but you are one crazy loon-toon lady, OK. *(Long pause. Lorna doesn't move. She appears frozen.)* I'm sorry. I didn't mean any offense, really. I just . . . I'm sorry I had a bad morning. I didn't mean to take it out on you. It's just none of them folks say they can even spare a dime or nickel. Come on. I know you had a hard childhood, but I had a hard night. I slept on a steam grate. And that's bad for your back. You got to go to a gynopractor to fix it. You see, my car ran outta gas here when I was visiting my sick . . . Are you OK? *(He whistles to try to get her eyes to follow him. He goes to touch her but she stands frozen.)* Oh, I'm very sorry. *(Bending down to look in her eyes.)* I hope I didn't do this to you. Hello? *(Waves his hand over her eyes.)* Hello? *(He looks at her.)* Hi. It's, it's just my car broke down and my mama is . . . *(She moans quietly.)* OK, OK, I'm lyin' OK. You're right. You got me. You called me out now. God's gonna get me too. I'm a little bit of an alcoholic, it's true, but I'm workin' on that. I didn't want to harm you now. I just. Ya know, I just, I just wanted a little bit of spare change. But that was rude. And I don't need it now. Especially since I know you're, no offense there, very, very mentally crazy. So I hope you're all right. I'm gonna go over by the store now. Nice talkin' to you. Have a good day. *(He starts to leave.)*

The Alien Hypothesis
By William Borden

Larry: any age, reflective, not outgoing

Seriocomic

Larry might be talking to a friend or to his psychotherapist. It's a quiet, private talk. Maybe they've asked him, "How are you feeling?" or "Is something bothering you?"

LARRY: Some people feel like they belong. I don't.
      I think I'm from outer space.
      No, listen, I'm not crazy. I'm merely entertaining hypotheses about the fact that I feel different. One hypothesis might be that I'm an alien from another planet, and I'm programmed not to realize this so I'll fit in, except the programming didn't work. Or else it did work, and I'm programmed to begin to realize the truth now. And at some time I will — I hope — receive further instructions. Maybe a manual, like you get with your DVD player, in twelve languages. I'm not looking for special privileges or anything. I'm just trying to find answers to these questions that keep popping into my head, like, "Who am I?" And "What am I doing here?" I suppose everybody wonders that, don't they?
      Maybe not.
      Even when I'm with other people who also feel different — you know, you're sitting around late at night discussing the meaning of life, and is God a Moslem or a Jew or an atheist, and you think, here's my club! We're all the same, we're all different! Until you realize you're even more different than the other different people.
      I've never seen a flying saucer. If I were really an alien, wouldn't they visit me? Just to say, Hi, Larry, how ya doin'? Keep up the good work . . . of being different. Well, they're busy. They're out there making crop circles, abducting humans.
      Hey! Are you out there? Why am I here? Are there others like me? What's the plan? Is there any meaning to it all? Where's the damn manual? I'm not alone, am I? Am I?

The Wet Science
By Benjamin Sahl

Frank: thirties, a sad, lost soul who has come to the Olympic trial to watch his brother compete . . . and maybe find a life.

Comic

Frank commiserates with, and competes with, Belle over who is carrying more emotional "baggage."

FRANK: I used to think I was growing — but I only felt bigger 'cause I was staying the same while my heart shrank, 'til I woke up one day and it was small enough I knew it couldn't hurt me no more. I can't remember what it's like to feel like I'm worth something. I'm dragging shit around with me from years. I'm like one a' those long-hair dogs gets its own shit caught in its fur on the back legs, dragging it around: I got shitlocks. Trailing behind me like a mile. I turn around, I can't see but one big black block a shit, blotting out the sun. Wish I could just snip a few hairs and leave it all behind. I mean, you can get lost in my shit. Jimmy Hoffa? That's right. I'm a fucking menace.

[BELLE: *After a certain point, it's so much easier to just drift toward death.*]

FRANK: In everything I do, there is this faint quality of bullshit. I can tell — I don't know how to get rid of it. It gets so all I want is for there to be a kind of clean neutral smell to everything. But objectively speaking, I'm an alright-looking guy, right?

Johnny Flip's Fate
By Chris Howlett

Fate: late thirties/ageless, frustrated overseer of infinite human destinies.

Seriocomic

Fate outlines to his clone ex-lover Anna why he is about to swap over the life of the eccentric human Johnny Flip and thus bring reality to an end for all time.

FATE: Why, Anna? Just have a fucking look around. Does this seem like a fulfilling existence to you? Do you think I enjoy watching these dumb creatures making their same dumb mistakes over and over again, no matter how much help they get? *(Pause.)*

I'm not even a Force with influence. What does Fate get to decide? Fate is about what has already been decided, isn't it? *(Beat.)* I'm a paper stamper. I'm a pen pusher. I'm a fucking transcendental Sisyphus. *(Beat.)* And the other Forces in this place never let me forget it either, fuckers! *(Pause.)*

I never asked for this shitty gig, Anna. I just got lumped with it for eternity. *(Beat.)* I'm better than this. I'm Fate.

Out of Place
By David Robson

Danny Dagan: thirties, Israeli police officer

Dramatic

> *Danny is interrogating a noted Palestinian-American scholar named Edmund Hassan on the suspicion of being an accomplice to a bus bombing. Edmund has just questioned the methods used by Danny, and others like him, to coerce confessions from suspects. Here Danny explains to Edmund how, when the stakes are so high, the ends always justify the means.*

DANNY: When survival is at stake everything changes. It has to, and that's when a secret world is activated — one where the press can't leak a story and where what we do to you doesn't get written down in any book. In other words, we blacken your eye — shhhh! We attach electrodes to your balls — it never happened in the first place. I know what you're thinking: This doesn't happen in a democracy. But that's where you're dead wrong. After 9/11 the U.S. finally woke up to what we've known for fifty years: If you want to fight them you have to join them. You have to come down from your ivory tower and get your hands dirty, use what they use, fight their fire with your fire, and make sure, most of all, that you don't lose. So fuck the false pride, Edmund. Take the first step and write the statement. Then we'll talk.

Erin Go Bragh-less
By John Shea

Barry: in his early thirties. Barry proclaims both his age and his love of beer on his puffy, ruddy face. Barry is one of the lucky few among us, for he is content with his lot in life. Harboring no great expectations, Barry sees no reason to upset the status quo, despite the changes around him. He selfishly pursues his own alcoholic and cocaine-filled pleasures regardless of the wife and children he neglects in doing so. Things are as they are, and Barry is more than willing to accept them, good or bad.

Dramatic

> *After a night of excessive drinking, Barry is trying to piece together the events of the night before, his having hit his wife and being told not to come home. Speaking to his friend, Bill, at Bill's house the next morning, Barry makes his decision not to change anything.*

BARRY: *(As he speaks, light slowly closes in on Barry, throughout his speech, he sips from the bottle, by the end, Barry holds the vodka bottle very tightly against his chest.)* Leave? So she can take me to court and I end up payin' child support while she's fuckin' around with Steve or God knows who else? No. They're my kids and she's my wife, that's how it's gonna stay. My kids aren't gonna be welfare rats, livin' on food stamps. I know what that's like. I remember how embarrassed I was usin' those fuckin' things, havin' everyone know, standin' in line for the free lunch tickets in school. She'd probly end up movin' back to the projects too. Livin' with the spics. That's who lives in the projects now, it's different than when I lived there. I'm stayin' home and she's stayin' with me. I want to know who's takin' care of my kids while I'm out bustin' my balls to make enough to finally live decently. I'm not fuckin' that up. I want my kids to know their father. I want them to know that I cared enough to stay around. And she's gotta be part of that. I'm not gettin' any divorce, see the kids when the judge tells me I can. Fuck that. We made this together and we're gonna stick with it. I see all these fuckin' losers, walkin' out on their wives, leavin' their kids to be beat up by the new boyfriend. I'll take care of my own kids. Otherwise they'll probly end up in jail. Look at my brother Ryan. A fuckin' junkie. And why? Because my fuckin' mother was out workin', not knowin' what was goin' on. If she was home where she belonged, none of this would have happened. And that's my father's fault for leavin', and I'm not gonna make the same mistake he made. And if that means I gotta keep knockin' Kelly up to make her stay home, then that's what I'll do. How she gonna survive without me with all those fuckin' kids, huh? And if she wanted to leave, I'd kick her fuckin' teeth down her throat and throw her out into the street and she'd never see those kids again. I'm a good father and she knows it. I never once hit those kids. *(Barry cradles bottle as light fades on him and Bill.)*

The Food Chain
By Keith Huff

Lou: thirties

Seriocomic

> *Lou is a hit man. He's riding in the passenger seat of a car*
> *with Jack, his . . . client, an Ivy League–schooled stockbro-*
> *ker in his late twenties who's borrowed and lost several hun-*
> *dred thousand dollars from Big Chunky, Lou's boss. Lou*
> *holds a gun. Jack's life is on the line . . . literally. But Jack is*
> *still young and cocky enough to think he's got the immor-*
> *tality market cornered and that he'll squirm out of this pinch*
> *somehow. Heck, he can't even say Big Chunky's name with-*
> *out cracking a smile. Lou tries his best to crack Jack's arro-*
> *gant facade.*

LOU: It's always been my motto to be on the lookout for the more substantial rewards life has to offer. I mean, you pop a guy in the kneecaps, the back of the head, the sadistic titillation, it comes, it goes with the heartless ferocity of a two-dollar hooker. Life should be about a little something more than that, don't you agree? *(Pause.)* You ever hear of Mad Sam Stefano, Jack? He was a little before your time maybe. Mad Sam was my mentor. What Merlin the Magician was to King Arthur, Mad Sam was to me. Mad Sam taught me every trick in the book. Mad Sam took some of the most inventive torture techniques — I'm talking way back to Inquisition times — and elevated them to an art form. He came up with ways to make a guy's pain last for weeks. Pain so intense, so relentless, if you handed the squid the appropriate means to do so, he'd pop himself on the spot, no hesitation. The only problem with Mad Sam was he enjoyed his work too much. Last guy he did, he nail gunned him by the earlobes, the webs of his fingers and toes to his workbench in the basement. Then he filled every one of his orifices with that expandable insulation foam that comes in the aerosol can. You know, the kind expands ten times its size and then turns to rock? Every living breathing one. Except his mouth. Mad Sam loved to hear 'em scream. It brought tears to his eyes. Tears of mirth. I witnessed this personally. And it became apparent to me, even at that tender age — I was sixteen or so — that even though Mad Sam truly enjoyed his work, here was a man who had plainly gone, as they say in the theatrical industry, over the top. So I popped him. It was a gesture of respect.

A Few Small Repairs
By David Robson

Quinton: thirties, ambitious town official

Seriocomic

> *Quinton and Hank — a police officer — are serving a search warrant on the ramshackle mansion of an eccentric old woman and her middle-aged daughter. Quinton suspects that the once aristocratic women are living in squalor and that their house should be condemned. Hank, on the other hand, is reluctant to get involved because he sees the women as helpless victims. Here Quinton reveals his contempt for following the rules as well as his naked ambition.*

QUINTON: Do you always play it right by the book, Hank? Don't you ever cut corners? Drop a dime? Trump the charges up a smidge? All you small-town cops have hard-ons about the book, but where I come from cops don't have the time to fill out a whole report. And when they want to get anything done the rules have to get tossed for a few minutes.

If the newspapers catch on, so be it. It wouldn't be the worst thing in the world. A reporter's job is to take a story and run with it, find the angles that will make the slack-jawed, life-addled reader turn to page twenty-six. You know why? Because on page twenty-six will be a half-page ad for women's underwear, so while the reader catches up on the news about the president's loony relatives, he can also stare to his heart's content at the 36DD brunette with the vacant stare and ass 'til Tuesday. This is how the newspaper makes its money; this is how a reporter earns his keep; and maybe — just maybe it's how the rest of us make friends and influence people — by supplying those stories.

There's nothing wrong with ambition is there? Last I heard it's the fuel this country ran on. Fall down a well — write a book about it. Get kidnapped by a band of Muslim extremists — sell it to ABC. Find yourself in a position of relative power — leverage what fate has placed in your clammy hands and see where the chips fall. Now, Hank, I think it's time for you to back off and let me handle this.

Whatever Happened to Godot?
By Jonathan Dorf

Man: twenties to thirties, a thinking thug

Comic

> *The monologue might be considered a twisted search for sympathy or commiseration. The baseball bat–wielding Man has arrived at the apartment where con artist Godot lives with the amnesiac Boy. Godot owes money, and the Man is the muscle. But Godot has bamboozled the Man into thinking Godot is his own butler. The Man, thinking in Godot he has found a fellow member of the working class, forces a bonding moment with him.*

MAN: Most people don't get it. They look at me like I'm some kinda' animal. I mean, here I am, a guy from a disadvantaged background attempting to improve myself — I'm taking classes, you know. But all I get is looked down on because I get my hands dirty. Example, this snot-nosed brat starts screaming words not even my mother — rest in peace — would have said, and biting me. Drawing blood even. I'm trying to snap his father's neck the most gentle and understanding way I know how, but all I get is this non-stop stream of abuse. Sure, the biting was bad — but it was the harsh words that left scars right here.
(Points to his heart.)
    I tried to explain how his dad owed money and wasn't being sensitive to my client's need to be close to it, but no. Yell yell yell, bite bite bite. You have no idea how much self-control it took not to off the little troll on the spot. I really wanted to. But I said to myself, no, that would be acting out of anger. And I do not want to be an angry man. So I made a calm, dare I say hopeful choice to cut his tongue out. My thought was if he had to listen to my point of view, maybe he'd understand, say "yes my friend, you're right." But he just kept spitting up blood. I felt like a failure.

How to Draw Mystical Creatures
By Ellen Margolis

Wolf: a Caucasian man in his mid-twenties to thirties. Usually soft-spoken, he is capable of chilling rage. He wears tennis shoes.

Dramatic

In his first appearance, Wolf addresses any secret predators who may be in the audience.

WOLF: There is a brief period — a matter of days, usually, and a week or two at most — when the mother has not yet started to think of her young as essential to her survival. Let her car engine catch fire, let an angry loner shoot up a Burger King, and she will run off in a panic for her own safety only. However she may have cooed over her squirming bundle of joy when he was first put to her breast, she will toss him to the devil as she would anyone else on earth until something – *something* — changes. After this point, the mother grows claws and teeth and will fight you to the death. But for those first few days, the opportunities abound. Candy from a baby.

Don't go looking for those opportunities. They are completely beside the point. The job, my job, your job, is to go to the edge of what is possible, beyond what is terrifying. They must never be able to rest, they must be made to understand that there is no safe place or time. That you will snatch a child from a crowded playground in the middle of the day or insert yourself into her snug pink bedroom in the middle of the night. They must be reminded and reminded and come to know that we are always there. To do your job properly, you have to pick the moments that are riskiest for you, the moments when no one in his right mind would dare to make a move.

They must be ready to organize a search party within hours. They must know where we are at any given moment, which is always right here. Here. HERE. NOW NOW. Only if they know *that* do we have a contest worthy of us.

A monster's not a monster unless it's right under the bed.

The Testimony of Gary Alan Richards
By Rohn Jay Miller

Gary Alan Richards: a hulking loser in his late thirties

Dramatic

> *Gary is having a boozy confrontation in front of family and friends with his ex-wife Linda at a party for their teen-aged daughter Kelly.*

GARY: Shut up, Linda. I got an announcement to make. Everybody listen! *(Stops, smiles slyly.)* I'm here to announce . . . the retirement of my friend, Rudy Brenner, from the bar business in the City of St. Paul. And the sale of the Sportsman's Bar . . . to me! Yeah! I'm going into the bar business for myself, Linda! And I don't put a dime down because Rudy's selling it to three of us — *on a note.* Yeah! We send him a check every month, and that's his retirement. Don't give me that look! It's completely on the level, Linda! And I can tell you why in two words: Rudy . . . Junior! Who's not the . . . *(Thinks.)* . . . sharpest pencil in the desk drawer, and his dad knows that. So Rudy Senior lives on the corner of *Rock and a Hard Place.* What's he gonna do? Sell the bar? How's Rudy Junior going to make sixty grand a year — and all the beer he can steal from the basement? Huh? Or — or! — he can bring in a grown-up to run the place with Rudy Junior. And I'm the grown-up, Linda. I talked him into it. Every month Rudy Senior gets a check for thirty-two hundred bucks, in Texas, or Mexico. Rudy Junior gets to keep his good job. And I own a bar. Yeah, Linda! I work twenty, twenty-five years, sell my share — and that's the end of the rainbow.

Untold Crimes of Insomniacs
By Janet Allard

The Entrepreneur: twenties to thirties; a kidnapper; a wild card. He runs his own designer kidnapping business, where people pay him for the thrill of being kidnapped.

Dramatic

In a van, in the middle of the night, two kidnappers: The Entrepreneur and his sidekick, dressed as a priest, wait till it's time to start the job. When the priest tries to quit on him, the Entrepreneur tries to scare him into staying — and living a life of risk.

ENTREPRENEUR: *(Entrepreneur points the gun at the priest.)* Tomato Macky. Macaroni and tomato sauce —
   Goulash. That's what it looks like. Brains.
   People look like puppets. When they're dead. You ever see a body?
   Puppets! One day SWACK your head goes flying off, you got a bullet through your heart, BLAM, a fence post through the windshield, SMACK. I used to watch my dad sew them together, embalm them, a piece here, a piece there, put back together a face, a leg, a skull, dress them up into their favorite clothes to hide the holes and missing parts. He looks me in the eye, square, like I'm staring at you now and says, son, you will never understand the line between the living and the dead.
   I'm your nightmare. I make a living at it. I've got fear to sell you, right here. Going cheap.
   Loose cannon, man, you are a loose cannon. That's who you are. Can't change it.
   Try to hide it, suppress it, close it up, shut it out, scare it away with reason. That's your fire. It's burning. Wild. It's wild it's hot and uncontained. Don't pretend, man. Put it on the line. Don't shut that down man, that'll kill you. You try to live a boring life. You're not cut out for it. You want to feel ALIVE!

Hay
By Cynthia Franks

Charlie: mid-thirties, long hair, lean, weather-worn, a tattoo. Charlie can be very charming when he wants to, but he can turn on a dime.

Dramatic

> *Charlie is speaking to Henry, the young man who's trying to save his mother's farm. Charlie stands to make a lot of money from the sale of the farm to developers and would like Henry to leave for good. Charlie is cleaning a rifle during this speech. The play is about the disappearing open lands in America.*

CHARLIE: You like the work you're doing? Fixing the place up? Help make it productive again, maybe? Good. Think you're doing the right thing? Saving the farm? You know what this land is worth to developers? My ma, could make a lot of money. She don't care, huh? Did I tell you my story about the dog and the train? I didn't? Well, I was down at the train station in Depot Town not too long ago passing time with friends when we heard these people yelling outside. A train had just gone through. These people come in saying we have to come and see this. I start to hear this wailing. It didn't sound like any living thing I ever heard. So we go. We get out there and there's this dog running around and these people are trying to catch it. I'm thinking what's the big deal? As we get closer, I see it's not a dog, but half a dog. I shit you not. Half a dog. The train hit it and cut it in two just around the hips. It cauterized it so it wasn't bleeding or nothing. This thing is running around screaming because these people are trying to help it. All it wants to do is lay down and die and these people won't leave it alone. I kept saying, "Someone shoot the thing." They told me I was a cold-hearted bastard. And these good-hearted people kept trying to help this half a dog. After about an hour the thing finally dropped. But it lived an hour of agony and terror it wouldn't have had to go through if the people would have left it alone. Let it die right where it should have. They had to agitate it. Keep it going. But the end was the same. Only it could've been much more peaceful. Let the dog die or you may see your hour of terror and agony. Do we understand each other? Good.

In the Coop
By Andrea Goyan

Sonny: thirty-three, an abusive alcoholic and generally feared by everyone he knows

Dramatic

> *Earlier in the evening, Sonny punched his wife Cindy in the face and broke her nose. He believes she is having an affair with a friend named Ronny. He now finds the two of them at a neighbor's house, where they are taking refuge, and confronts them.*

SONNY: Honey, you're sure a mess. You should go home and clean up. You seem to have blood all down the front of that new white blouse. You really should get it in some water right away. I like the way that blouse looks on you. Sort of makes you look like the whore you are. Oh, wait, you ain't smart enough to get paid for giving it out. If you were maybe we'd have a few extra dollars. No, you like to give it away. Or maybe you give it away because the trash who'd take you never have any money anyway. *(He turns to Ronny.)* If you never pay for beer, how can I possibly expect you to pay for my wife? Drop your pants. Or maybe you only respond when my wife asks you to do it. Go ahead, Cindy, let me hear how you'd say it. Did she ask you real sexy like or did she just go ahead and help you take them off? Huh? Huh, Ronnie, huh? Oh, my imagination is running wild. I keep seeing the way my wife is with me but then suddenly it's your face she's kissing. I'm thinking all sorts of crazy things. Take off your pants! Good boy. Go through your pockets . . . all of them. What's that you're trying to hide? Open your fist, naked boy, before I kick your ass. Well, lookie there, ten big ones. Ronnie's been holding out all this time. All them pitchers of beer and lover boy never bought one. I thought he was broke, turns out he's just cheap.

Grunions
By Barbara Lindsay

Augie: thirties, is a good-hearted man, simple in his needs and pleasures, and much more knowing than he appears to be. He is devoted to his temperamental wife, Carla.

Comic

Augie and Carla, a married couple, have come to the beach at midnight to watch the running of the grunion.

AUGIE: We weren't in a good spot last year. This is a much better spot. I've got good instincts for these things. Look there, what's that? Is that . . . ? Is that . . . ? No, that's seaweed, isn't it. Oh man, this is great. I wouldn't miss this for anything. I mean, think about this. I know you're not interested, but just think about this for a minute. Out there someplace, there's this huge mass of silver fish heading this way. They don't know why. We don't know why. It wasn't a decision, they didn't take a vote, no one sent them an invitation or a map. Just some little instinctual time-release firecracker went off in their bodies, and all as one, they turned and formed a line as long as the California coast, and started swimming. They're swimming right now, as if that's the only thing that matters. It's single-mindedness with no mind, urgency that's pure urge. They don't know what drives them; they don't give it a name or ask it a question. They just turn as one and start the swim that brings them here, to this place where we stand, for a massive celebration of sex and death. Look at this, I'm giving myself goose bumps. All my hairs are popping up. Well, so what do you think?

The Line Shack
By Kevin M. Lottes

Ralph Roberts: a man in his mid-thirties

Seriocomic

> *Ralph is a pilot about to conduct an air show at a small, private airline company. He finds himself in the aircraft refuelers' lounge room, waiting for his plane to get refueled. In the midst of waiting, he runs into a few, young aircraft refuelers who feel stuck in a routine that they can't escape from. One young refueler used to dream of being a pilot like Ralph, but finds himself still refueling planes; another yearns to be a writer but never seems to find the time to write anything. Ralph tries to motivate them to make choices, to take risks, and to accept the ramifications of those choices in order to achieve their dreams.*

RALPH: Conducting an air show is the absolute greatest rush of adrenaline that I've ever experienced in all my years of flight. It's like all your years of training and all your hours of flying put to the ultimate test. Like a playful dogfight. It's amazing. The sky turns into this very narrow field of blue where the room for error gets smaller and smaller. The sky is no longer the limit. It's the sky now that limits you because you have to manage this tiny fleet of planes — I mean it's not tiny to me — but to the sky, it's a small basket of apples to juggle. I can't use the whole sky; the choices that can be made up there are overwhelming. I mean I just don't have the resources to use all of it. But still, choices have to be made. I have this and that's it. That's what I have to work with you know? So once we're all up in the air and they all start following your lead they all become *your* responsibility in a sense. And if you mislead just one of them, just one of them, the whole scene could come crashing down on you like hot blueberry bird shit smacking down on your windshield as you're drivin' home from work after one shitty day at your one pitiful little job after another. To be up there, up for grabs like that, is the greatest rush of all and I wouldn't settle for anything less than the tallest sky to climb. Hot damn! I'm ready! Is he ready yet?

4 Murders
By Brett Neveu

Mitch: twenty-five to thirty-five, a mid-level workaholic business-man

Seriocomic

Mitch has just let a possible food-delivery person, Joel, into his office. Upon Joel's entrance, Mitch attempts to engage him in conversation to relieve his own boredom and feed his curiosity. Fascinated, Mitch asks questions regarding his own current insertion into Joel's nightly routine, hoping to find some excitement therein.

MITCH: You just began your shift, then? Wait. Am I the first delivery of your first day on your new delivery job? If so, that is amazing, that is amazing, if I'm your first. If I am, you'll remember me, then, I bet you'll remember me, years from now, you'll remember me when you think back on the time you had a delivery job and you'll remember your first delivery and it will be me that you think of. I don't mind if I'm that person and actually, to tell you, I can't believe it's me. That sort of thing rarely happens in life, being remembered in someone's tale of whatever that tale may be, and in your case, the tale of when you first delivered on your first day as a delivery person, if in fact I'm your first. If so, I'm a part of that story. And if so, it would be quite a nice surprise.

4 Murders
By Brett Neveu

Mitch: twenty-five to thirty-five, a mid-level workaholic business-man

Seriocomic

Mitch is speaking to Joel, a man whom he perceives to be a food-delivery person. It being late and it being Joel's last delivery, Mitch convinces Joel to sit down in his office and speak with him for awhile. Comfortable with Joel after a few minutes of conversation, Mitch attempts to engage Joel with an outrageous "what-if" situation that he thinks both of them will surely find hilarious.

MITCH: I wish, hold on, this would be funny, wait, this would be funny don't you think? I wish, I wish that you and I, or some-body or you or I, I wish we could go down there and so we're outside, we're talking or smoking cigarettes and we're standing right outside and we're standing and the fumes, the fumes from the beer truck spill, the beer fumes, they are so strong that in that moment we are standing outside we become suddenly and vio-lently drunk, falling-down drunk, laughing and grabbing women by their chests and we're very, very, very drunk, we are falling-down drunk. And it's just because of the beer fumes in the air and not because we drank any alcohol. So it wouldn't be our fault that we were drunk because we were just outside and hap-pened to be breathing near the spot where the beer truck had spilled thousands of bottles of beer on the ground and that's what made us drunk. But not by drinking any beer at all. How about that? That would be funny and very unexpected for passerby and individual, don't you think?

If This Isn't Love
By Jonathan Bernstein

Hank: thirty-one, a part-time college student and test subject for pharmaceutical research

Seriocomic

> *Hank and his girlfriend Katie have taken two pregnancy tests this evening; they've both been positive. In this scene, Hank returns to the pharmacy for a third time to buy yet another test. He's slowly reconciling the prospect of pending fatherhood as he chafes at the smirk on the cashier's face.*

HANK: Hi, I'm back. I figured I'd just for the hell of it go ahead and purchase another one of these little pregnancy tests. I have exact change this time . . . Third time's the charm.

My girlfriend's flipping out a bit, just a little bit. You know. I don't know. You know what? No, this is going to be OK, it's not a bad thing. It's pretty beautiful, actually, we're going to make a child. It's better than beautiful, it's out of sight and it's going to be fine — it's going to be great. I'm going to find a steady salary in a job with health insurance, and I'm going to . . . goddamn it, I'm going to do my taxes. That's what I'm going to do. And I'm going to build a crib, and paint clouds on the walls, and I'm not going to care what clothes get spit on or what anyone says, it doesn't matter what other people've done or how they've done it because this is ours and this is how we're going to go about it and you watch, man, we're going to be great together. I'm telling you, I'm going to hold that kid so tight, I'm going to protect the hell out of him, or her. I'm going to be happy. We're going to be happy. We're going to be so goddamn happy, you wait and see. You watch. This's going to be great.

Big Night
By N. M. Brewka

Richard: male in his late twenties to mid-thirties

Dramatic

> *Richard, a recent Ph.D. in botany, is asking his longtime
> girlfriend Lana, a doctoral candidate in art history, to take a
> leave of absence to go to Yemen with him for a year of post-
> doctoral research.*

RICHARD: I'm moving. To Yemen. For a year. It all happened really,
really fast. Dr. Krishiztsky did all the paperwork. I never thought
they'd buy it, a post-doc in an Arab state, but he's got pull in
D.C. and somehow it all came together. I thought maybe Terry
would've said something. I'm going to study Catha edulis. Qat.
(Pronounced 'cot.') Otherwise known as Mirra, Tohai, Abyssin-
ian Tea, African Salad. I'm supposed to find out how it grows
over there so we can grow it here, we being the U.S. government.
What the goal is, I have no idea. I just know the botanical
aspects. It's a Class Four drug for forty-eight hours, then drops
way down the baddie scale. Maybe it's supposed to replace the
bong, or the martini. *(Pause.)*
  Lana, you have no idea how much effort Krishiztsky put
into this. He thinks when I come back, there'll be a department
chair with my name on it. Between his retirement and all the
heavy-duty cuts in the state budget, somebody's got to survive
and thrive. Lana, sweetheart, listen to me. That's going to be me.
But I don't want to go without you. I'm asking you to take a
leave of absence and come with me. You can study over there.
Lana, please. I love you.

Pitchin' Pennies at the Stars
By Jeanette D. Farr

Vincent: late twenties to early thirties, an optimist who's trying to
"make it" in Hollywood as a writer

Seriocomic

*Vincent, an optimist whose life revolves around "movie
moments," explains his view on the perfect woman.*

VINCENT: You know what one quintessential movie depicts what it all
means and why I'm in this wacky business? *It's a Wonderful
Life.* Nobody could compare to the angel in that movie. No! Not
Clarence! Sure, he's the guy who shows Jimmy Stewart what it
was like if he was never born, but I'm not talking about that
angel, but the angel of cinema: Donna Reed! The first time she
and Jimmy Stewart kiss, it's magic. They've got Sam Wanewright
on the phone and Mom's upstairs and they're looking into each
other's eyes, kinda sideways, but cheek to cheek. Sam's on the
phone, blah, blah, blah, and they're just lookin'. He's lookin' at
her, she's lookin' at him and you know in that one look — that
one instant — they want it. He wants her, and oh, boy, does she
want him. Then he grabs her, right? Totally manhandles her then
gives her the "what for." George Bailey wants so damn bad to
get out of Bedford Falls — the world is his oyster, he can travel
all over, but no he doesn't do it, because you know what's keeping him there? Huh? *(As if it's obvious.)* He wants to MAKE IT
WITH DONNA REED! And who wouldn't? What a woman.
That moment — that's not someone's creation. That moment is
real — captured in cinema and preserved for all the world to see.

The Art of the Forecast
By Dennis Schebetta

Larry: a TV weatherman

Comic

> *Larry has been sitting half-naked on a chair for the past two hours, posing for his girlfriend, Harmony, who has been painting his portrait. She hopes tonight he will want to stay over for the first time. He just hopes the portrait is good. But the painting is atrocious and he is cornered into giving his opinion.*

LARRY: *That* took you two hours? I mean . . . I . . . I . . . I like it. It's so . . . It's different. I'm sorry. No one's ever done an abstract portrait of me before and I don't know the right words here. I can't exactly say "Wow! It looks just like me!" What, you want my insignificant and may I mention, *uninformed,* opinion? OK. Fine. Here goes . . . *(Takes a deep breath.)*
  First of all, you cut off my head! My head is floating in some ethereal, nonspecific space! It appears to have been violently ripped off the neck. See the jagged edges here at my throat done in blood red. Who did you take art lessons from? Charles Manson? And I'm a little angry about freezing my ass off sitting naked in that chair for two hours just so that you could do a portrait of only my floating discombobulated head! And, y'know, as a whole package for the eyes it doesn't — It doesn't have — *Colors!* Paintings should be like a symphony of color, right? And you have, one, two, three, *four* colors there. Not to mention that your technique is crude — look at the crooked brushstrokes — and this is coming from a guy who learned to use the word *technique* in a sentence only a few weeks ago. The fact that you imagine some aspect of my personality as a mutilated head floating in space doesn't concern me as much as the fact that this thing was such a huge disappointment. Two hours and this is the great masterpiece? A preschooler could do a better finger painting than this lazy excuse for a picture. *(Beat.)*
  Is this too much? I'm sorry, I'll stop.

Bridewell
By Charles Evered

Bridewell: late thirties to forties, a telephone repairman

Comic

Bridewell relates a personal story to a room full of sorority girls.

BRIDEWELL: Well, let me tell you something. My first wife, within seven months of marrying me, went from being a delightful, shapely, cheerful young gal I knew from the neighborhood to being a fat pig. Now, I know it's not politically whatever ya call it to say it like that, but there was no other way to describe her. I remember rolling over one morning and looking at her — a whole slab of her cheek taking up half the pillow and me shaking her awake — looking her right in the eye and saying; "Baby, you are a fat pig." And so off we go to some kind of psycho-ologist or whatever ya want to call it dot head doctor she heard about who starts rattling off this bull crap about *(In an offensive Indian accent.)* "Oh, psychological transference . . ." or some such bull crap like that and I hold up my finger like this and I say; "Doc, ya know what? Let me ask you something: If my wife didn't eat twelve times her body weight in Oreos every day, would she still be fat?" *(In offensive dialect.)* "Oh, but you do not understand the underlying . . ." and I hold up my finger again and I say; "No, Doc . . . *you* don't understand. See, the problem with fat people? *(Almost in a whisper.)* They eat too much."

Rights to Act
By Dominic Taylor

Pete: thirties, African-American

Dramatic

> *Pete has come to visit his only son, Rasuol, at his estranged common-law wife's home. He has heard that his son has been talking to a treacherous man known as Knox.*

PETE: I'ma tell you this once. You getting to an age where you making some moves, but with me, you ain't got no choice. What I'm telling you is simple. They ain't never locking you up, if I can help it.

You ain't gonna be playing on the side of the illegal, or with nobody who is. You ain't gonna get a jay-walking ticket if I can help it.

(Pulls out a .38 and puts it to Rasuol's head.)

I'm not playing with you boy. You hear me?

(Rasuol says nothing.)

All you got in this life is time. I'm your father, so if you think, I'ma let the state trick you outta your time? Nah, you wrong. You think I'ma let Knox bullshit get you to run out and do some dumb shit, and end up doing a bid? No son. You know me. I did seven; your mother just finished her dime, that's enough time by the whole family. Now some of your boys, ain't like you. You got a mother and a father who can school you. Neither one of us perpetrating on this. We paid so you won't have to. Anybody smells, the least bit funky, you stay away.

The Great Hugo Barnes
By Dennis Schebetta

Hugo: twenties to thirties, a reclusive armchair philosopher

Seriocomic

> *In his apartment in Hell's Kitchen, Hugo reluctantly gives advice to Kate, one of his upstairs neighbors who is in a tempestuous relationship with Scott. She has literally forced herself into his apartment thinking Scott has been hiding there and Hugo has desperately been trying to get her to leave him alone but to no avail, so he finally unleashes one last tactic — cold, blunt truths.*

HUGO: Kate, I'm trying not to be rude. You're a sweet lovely girl with a cute smile, a fiery temper, and ample breasts. However, your taste in men, particularly Scott, leaves something to be desired. You constantly pick the wrong man to be with and then cry a regular river of tears over the mess that develops because of it. This is insane, illogical behavior. It's like you're addicted to the drug of stupidity. If there's a stupid man on the planet you want to try it, kiss it, swallow it, take it home and fuck it. I advise you to take a long look at yourself in the mirror, clean out all of your old photo albums, buy yourself a new wardrobe, and move on with your life. In short: Get smart.
(Beat.)
     I hope that helped you. No thanks are necessary. Now good day.

(a) Dream in an Airport
By Adam Simon

Nestor: a drunken pilot in his thirties

Comic

> *Owen Flobert has been tossed around in an airport in a
> ridiculous and satirical security scare. It is late at night in an
> airport bar when he encounters Nestor, an unapologetically
> drunk pilot who seeks to give advice to another weary trav-
> eler. Nestor has just asked Owen if he's going to get
> switched to another flight. Owen replies "I'm going to check
> on it." Nestor prods "Oh yeah, when?" Owen simply says
> "Soon."*

NESTOR: Lemme give you a little tip, go to the broads at the gate, not
the ones in the front area there. They don't have their supervisor
right there and if you say what you're after with a little force,
more often than not it's yours. And you don't have to yell. Who
said yell? I'm not saying yell at 'em.

Just let them know what you want. Some people are so
polite here, like an airport's any different from a fast-food joint
or something. They get their tickets and they're prim and all that
shit, and then they go to get some food two steps away and
they're like "gimme this" and "get me some salt" like the two
places are any different. It's about how you ask. If you ask like
a little kid, you'll get treated like one. You gotta ask like a man
and they'll have no choice but to say yes. Helen knows what I'm
talking about.

*(Helen gives him a look. Finishes her martini, picks up her bag
and walks away muttering under her breath.)*

NESTOR: Take her for example. I mean I did. *(Slight chuckle at his
own joke.)* She slept with me because I'm a pilot. Why do cheer-
leaders sleep with football players? Because they're pilots. This
place is no different than any other place. You keep that in mind.
You better. Otherwise you'll be here for a while.

The Moment of Truth
from *Crazyology*
By Frank Higgins

Brad: thirty-three, handsome

Comic

At a bar, Brad helps a male friend out by telling him how to seduce married women.

BRAD: I've got a lot of married women friends, and they all think I'm real insightful. Now no relationship I've ever been in has ever worked out, and I can never figure out why it goes bad, so why do my female friends think I'm insightful? *Because* a lot of times I call them up and say "Hi, how you doing?" And they say fine, and I pause and say:

"You OK?" "What do you mean?" "You sound different somehow. Are you alright?"

And almost always they're *not* alright. They're unhappy about something with their husbands or their boyfriends, and within just a few seconds of telling me they're alright, they're telling me how miserable they are.

"And you could see all that. You could tell that in just a few seconds."

And I say, "Well, I'm just looking out for you."

And they say, "You *know* me. You can see right inside me."

And I say, and this is the moment of truth, but you gotta cover yourself, give yourself room to maneuver, "Well I'm sure it's nice inside you."

Now what's she say next? *If* she gets cold and says "What-ta you mean?" you can say, "There's a great person inside you," and you're safe. *But* . . . keep in mind most married women don't get flattered or flirted with by their husbands anymore, so she'll probably take a moment and then say, "Would you like to have lunch tomorrow?" And you're in.

Don't believe me? Try it. Call up some married woman you know, and start to talk about one thing, and then stop and ask, "Are you OK?" And don't take yes for an answer.

Pitchin' Pennies at the Stars
By Jeanette D. Farr

Carmine: late thirties, the stereotype of the Italian Mafia, but a teddy bear through and through, loves coffee and his daughter, Loni, he's very big on family

Comic

Carmine, a man of Italian descent with a Mafia flair, tells his nephew Vincent how a certain moment in the movies changed his life.

CARMINE: Life isn't like the movies, Vincent. In fact, the people who make those pictures don't know nothin' about loyalty. You don't believe me? OK, fine, get this then. One minute I'm havin' a great dinner with the family. The next minute my mother is crying and says we need to get the hell to the movie house before the cops come. So me and my brother, Geno, go to see this supposedly happy story about a boy and his dog. The kid finds this big yellow dog and he makes friends with it and this dog does everything for him — saves his life from a bear and everything — true devotion, right? During the middle of the picture, I have to go to the can. I didn't wanna leave, but when you gotta go, you gotta go. So I get done doin' my business, and when I get back, the kid's got a rifle pointed at the dog. *(Choking up.)* What is with THAT?? They call it a classic — a "family story." They CALL it *Old Yeller* after the dog — but they ought to call it "Boy Fucking Shoots an Old Yellow Dog" so you know what you're getting into. I tell ya, I wasn't the same after that.

Hurricane Iris
By Justin Warner

Job: a Biblical apparition, thirties

Seriocomic

> *It is near sundown at the end of Yom Kippur, the time of atonement. Job, the Biblical antihero, has appeared to Nell, a female rabbi, after she strangles her comically abusive mother. Stung by Nell's recent rejection of his self-sacrificing agenda, Job now tells Nell about the divine retribution that's in store for her.*

JOB: You know something, Nell? You're more naïve than I thought you were.

You think Yom Kippur is all about getting into the Book of Life? Please. The Book's a showpiece. You know as well as I do what happens at sundown: nothing. There's no bell or buzzer going off. There's no report card. There's just that grating, nagging voice inside your head that says everything you've ever done isn't good enough. That's God's secret weapon. It's pre-installed in every Jewish brain since the fall of Adam. It's more powerful than any of the external crap I've had to put up with. You want wrath?

(He points to his own temple.)

That's where the wrath is. And it never goes away. You can't kill it. Even if you turn away from God, the voice keeps on coming back. Which is just the way God likes it because He hates to be ignored.

[NELL: *If I just had another chance . . . I didn't think I would actually kill her . . .*]

JOB: Sacrifice and atonement. That's the only salve.

And you're going to need plenty of it when the sun goes down tonight! You've never been smited like the Lord's gonna smite you now!

Finding Faith
from *Skin & Bone*
By Lisa Rosenthal

Dean: thirty-six. Dean has been around the block a few times, knows how to give women what they want, and has no problem giving it to them so he gets what he wants, which is to get laid.

Comic

Dean is explaining the facts of life to a younger man in a bar.

DEAN: That's why I like them young — less cynical. When I tell a young woman she's beautiful, she believes me. I've been around so it means more to her. Now if I tell an older woman she's beautiful, she'll think I'm up to something; trying for a ticket to heaven. And I am. Aren't we all? Because when you get right down to it, life is all about getting off. *(Beat.)*
    You make a woman feel desirable . . . beautiful, and she will *be* delicious. That's the key. They will become downright religious — feeling blessed for having you in their life (if only for a night), sing praises for your inspiring words, kneel and pray at the temple of your generous spirit. And give head. Make a woman feel beautiful and she will give you a ticket to paradise.

The Cost of Mathematics
By L. Pontius

TED: thirty-two, a mathematics teacher at a high school

Dramatic

> *Ted has been sleeping with one of his students, who is now*
> *pregnant. She and her boyfriend are blackmailing him. Ted*
> *has come to her house with the money to confront them.*

TED: *(Ted puts a bag at his feet.)* I don't want to get upset. I could have taken this money. I could have left; I could have disappeared. But I'm not doing that. I got the money. It's for you. You and Susan. To start a new life. You, her, the baby. Far away as you want from me. I just want to see Susan first.

Look, my wife is sitting in the car waiting to go to the mall, she thinks I'm being nice and lending a student of mine some luggage. I'm giving you two fucking teenagers twenty thousand dollars and Susan's sitting in her room? Fuck that. She needs to show her face. HER FACE. Her lovely little face.

Paul, she's not happy. She's angry with me. She needs to know . . . she needs to stand in front of me and I can tell her how sorry I am. Susan and I can work this out.

I can make her happy again.

I'll put it to you simply. You're not getting this money until I see her, Paul. You go and tell your girlfriend, that if she doesn't come out here and face me you're not going to get this money. If Susan says no, fine, fine, I'll walk off this porch and tell my wife right now that I fucked one of my students, and then I'm going to tell her, this twenty thousand dollars, it's for Susan, she's blackmailing me, blackmailing both of us. So, go ahead Paul, make a choice, get your girlfriend out here, and get twenty thousand dollars, or get nothing.

The Mushroom Treatment
By Adam Simon

Miles: thirties, extremely confident, successful, white, archetypal-
   looking

Seriocomic

> *Miles has left his job as a CEO of a very lucrative company
> to run for president in a formerly war-torn African nation.
> He has just learned that his campaign vans are being shot at
> as they drive around town with his picture and his speech
> coming from their speakers. He plans his next moves with
> Dave, his campaign manager.*

MILES: I think it's important to stay "on issue" here and anything that
   can distract attention from the issue isn't going to help, Dave.
   Don't be afraid to be blunt with this thing. Spell it out: You're a
   poor and starving nation, you need leadership, you need eco-
   nomic growth and foreign investment, and then, you know,
   point out that I'm the only candidate among the — what are
   there like thirty now — that's why we have to stay on message
   here. There's a sea of candidates and I'm the only white face in
   the crowd. I'm the only American face in the crowd. We can't
   let that become an issue, we can't let anything become an issue
   here that is not of our choosing you know?

St. Colm's Inch
By Robert Koon

John: thirty-nine

Dramatic

> *John is in the house of his deceased ex-wife. He is speaking to her sister, who has come to help pack up the effects and is reluctant to accept any hospitality.*

JOHN: Did . . . did she ever tell you . . .

    The last time I was here, the last time before . . . when Marie was alive was the day I moved out. I moved out in garbage bags. Those big, green garbage bags. Didn't pack, just threw my stuff in and . . . and we were fighting, yelling at one another about . . . who knows . . . I was . . . drunk, probably . . .

    And I was headed out the door and she grabbed me, and I pulled away, and she fell . . .

    I didn't push her.

    I don't think I pushed her.

    And . . . I was at the door and I turned back, and . . . she was there, on the floor, and I . . . I just wanted to hurt her. I wanted to . . . I told her I ought to burn down this house, with her in it. And I didn't mean it, and *she* knew I didn't mean it, but I couldn't stop myself. And I couldn't believe I'd said it. What a low thing to say. How could anyone . . . And I saw her face, and I knew that just by saying it I had lost . . .

    I didn't mean it. And I never told her. I mean, we never talked all that much after, and when we did, it was never the right time, and then . . . and then you were putting her in the ground and now there'll never be a right time. And when I found out she left this place to me, I thought "what perfect revenge." On me. Perfect.

    So it's here, and . . . if you want to stay here . . .

    I just need to settle up, OK?

A Good Solid Home
By Barbara Lhota and Janet B. Milstein

Robert: thirties, a corporate lawyer

Dramatic

> *Robert, thirties, and his wife adopted a boy from a young mother several months ago. In the recent weeks, the baby's birth mother, Angie, has begun contacting the couple who lives in Florida. This evening, she has traveled from New Jersey to visit the adoptive parents. In this speech, Robert tries to convince Angie that her choice to give up her baby to them was a solid one.*

ROBERT: I don't mean that about you. It's just, it's difficult to explain how hard it is. And I don't feel it necessary to describe the details to everyone. Suffice to say that it's full of hospitals, and incredible amounts of time, and money, procedures, and discussions, and decisions, and heart breaks. We are all taught that having a child is a natural occurrence — anyone can do it. Anyone . . . but *you.* Each attempt gets your hopes up. And worse, you carry the hopes of all your friends and family with you. Each time it fails, you feel like a deficient human being. You feel that God is against you. That you don't deserve what others receive so naturally. It keeps, it keeps making you feel less than you are over and over. I'm sorry to go on about it. *(Beat.)* The thing is we have so much to offer your son, Angie. And I don't mean just material things, although that makes life easier, but I mean a solid home, a wealth of experiences, and a sense of who we are. Things you haven't even given yourself enough chance to develop yet. If you only knew how much of a family we are already, you wouldn't even consider this. What a kid needs is for you to give him a sense of accomplishment, which only happens after *you've* accomplished things you're proud of in your own life. You're so young, Angie. You'll have another chance. Plenty of them. I know it. And by that time, you'll have so much more to share.

Last Love
By Peter Papadopoulos

Charles: late twenties to early thirties, an overly intellectual, unsuccessful business manager

Dramatic

On the eve of their three-year wedding anniversary, Lucida flies into a rage after Charles once again forgets to put the toilet seat down after using the bathroom. Lucida then goes on to criticize Charles for his other shortcomings. Here Charles responds by telling Lucida that he doesn't want to be married to her any more.

CHARLES: In the beginning
there was appreciation
and congratulations
on fixing the porch
or at least trying to fix the porch — I still haven't finished — I know!
And trimming the hedges
even if I didn't do such a good job
because I'm not really the type of man
who is very good at these kinds of things
but I wanted to be
for you
for us
and to hear you say
thank you, Charles,
you did a wonderful job on the hedges
made three hours of struggling
sweat pouring down my face
my arms cut and bleeding
my shirt ruined
worthwhile
and I felt proud
and like a man
in the way that a man wants to be thought of by his wife.

And by himself.

Because growing up
I was never that kind of boy
my father would stand over me
hollering about how badly I was trimming the hedges
wrench the shears from my hands
and leave me to watch
while he snapped at the bushes
with iron ramrod precision
"Like this! Like this!"
while I stood
small and twisted
the tattered cloth remains of an airplane seat
fluttering in the trees above the fuselage
my punishment
to watch in humiliation
for not doing it right the first time.

And now
to finish the hedges
and sense your disapproval . . .
what's the difference?

I know I am a man who has been doing his best —
but the desire has gone out.
To do my best for you
because no matter how hard I work
to get the nails just right in the porch
I will hear
in your thank you
the disapproval
that comes from the understanding
the unshakable belief
that you married a loser
someone not to be proud of
because he really can't get the nails straight
even after ruining scores of them
bending them blindly
one after another

frustrated
angry
swollen-thumbed
and struggling
to do this one small thing right.
As if in this act
I could win back your respect.

Your love.

Last Love
By Peter Papadopoulos

Jim: late twenties to early thirties, a soft-spoken construction worker

Dramatic

> *Seven years ago Jim and Sally's relationship came to an abrupt end when Jim failed to call Sally for their next date as promised, and Sally refused to give in and call him to see what was wrong. When coincidence reunites them many years later, Sally launches an all-out assault on Jim for not calling. Here Jim gathers his courage and reveals to Sally the real reason he never called her.*

JIM: I wanted to marry you.
But only if you were the kind of person who would call me when I didn't call you.
That I could let you down
once in a while
and that would still be OK.

That I didn't have to be perfect
infallible
one hundred percent reliable
and when I wasn't
that YOU would, maybe,
reach out to ME.

My mother always did the reaching out
and my father scorned her for it
thought she was weak
couldn't make it on her own.
He would rather go a month of silence
than make that first gesture
because he thought this was strength.

And I guess part of me
came to think of this as strength, too.

Well, perhaps,
but at least,
that if I were to marry you
which I deeply wanted to do
I didn't want to always have to be the one doing the reaching out
holding the pieces together.
Not always.

Because I think
in the beginning
this can be thought of as sweet
and courageous
and strong and manly even
to be the one who has the courage to do this.
But
I think
in my experience
in time
this person becomes regarded as
a doormat
trampled all over
for his efforts
to keep the relationship connected.

I just
didn't want to become a doormat.
That's why I'm good with my hands
with tools.
That way I'll always be needed
even if I' m not necessarily wanted.

(Pause.)

But what I really want
what I really need
is to be
needed

even if I'm NOT useful
or one hundred percent reliable.

Let a Hundred Flowers Bloom
By David Zellnik

Puppy: thirty-two

Dramatic

> *Puppy, a disabled gay guy, has taken in his best friend Jake*
> *who a month ago went off his AIDS drugs in a suicide*
> *attempt. He has nursed Jake back to health from the side*
> *effects of going off his meds (and the depression that led him*
> *to do so) but now better, Jake has decided to go back to the*
> *boyfriend he left in the first place. The boyfriend takes him*
> *back . . . that is until Puppy tells him about all the affairs*
> *Jake has been having in the past month. Jake is furious, and*
> *Puppy admits the reason he's trying to break up Jake and*
> *Samson for good is because he himself is in love with Jake.*
> *Jake lashes out "How dare you do this to me?! You're my*
> *best friend!" Puppy responds.*

PUPPY: How dare I what — *help you?* Take you in and *love you* and watch you get better and then watch you run away cause you're scared of what's going on between us? Maybe I don't *want* to be your fucking best friend anymore. Maybe I'm tired of that role. Maybe I've called my agent and asked to be sent out for leading man roles OK? Maybe the best friend narrative is *tiring.* Maybe I'm not always *rooting* for you, you know, on your little adventures. And yes, I don't know the best ways to do these things because I never went through the learning process when I was eighteen and that's not my fault. But I do know what we have is real, and why shouldn't I fight for it, dirty and mean if I have to? Please stay. I want you to stay. To sleep with me, to have sex every night at first, then every other night, then twice a week, then once a week. I want to be an old married couple with you. I want to be . . . *(Ashamed.)* bourgeois.

Romance
By Barbara Lhota

Mick: thirties, a mail carrier

Dramatic

Mick, thirties, explains to Miriam, a woman he's only just met in this chapel in the middle of the night, how he was jilted at the altar today.

MICK: The family was spread over the pews. He isn't Catholic exactly, but close enough. The brothers and sisters, all married, sat right here. And there . . . *(He points.)* There sat Mom, hair done up high. So they do the whole walk down the aisle, everything's smooth. Everybody's pretty. Until they get to the part where ya got to, where ya gotta . . . *(Slaps his hand.)* Wham! You know, tell it like it is. And he gets to askin' her if she wants to spend the rest of life with him and there's this pause. And he thinks — "Wow, she's makin' this dramatic!" But the pause goes on. He looks over at her and she doesn't move. She stands there. Still. Only he can hear her breathing. He tries to catch her eye to see if she's just nervous, but she ignores him. He looks over at Mom and her forehead's all wrinkled, tense, and her hair starts unraveling. And then, this knot forms in his throat — like a lump, but kinda twisted, and it gets real dry. And he thinks, he can say something, do something, tell a joke, he can stop this. But the only thing that comes out of his mouth is a little moan. A little cry — a noise, so small. You can barely understand that he's sayin' "Marie, Marie." She turns to him with a face so full up of sorry. His sisters, his brother keep tellin' him that it was cold feet — cold feet. But in that instant, he knew she didn't love him. She wanted, wished, hoped to, but she just didn't. She wanted to, but she didn't. Didn't love him. And the whole thing turned into a Goddamn funeral. *(Pause.)* So don't tell me about lonely.

Whispers in the Wind
By Melissa Gawlowski

Tom: a priest in his early thirties

Dramatic

> *Tom, who is doing missionary work in a foreign country,
> has just been rebuffed by another prospective convert. Feel-
> ing lonely and disenchanted, he begs God to renew his sense
> of purpose.*

TOM: I want you to understand. I'm not asking for proof. I'm not
doubting, it's just — Did I ever tell you about this? The first time
I really saw you. I was . . . probably twelve, thirteen . . . and I
noticed you looking at me from across the room. Don't ask me
how I knew it was me you were watching, but . . . it was in your
eyes. Your eyes. God, so beautiful, so . . . full. You saw all the
way inside me. It was so overwhelming, all of it — the music
beating, voices singing, so much emotion, incense making my
head whirl, and you, there, amongst it all, but quiet. Watching
me. And without a word, I knew you understood everything, my
confusion, frustration, my loneliness. And I never wavered from
you. Not one moment since. Do you realize that? Fifteen years
now — I gave you my life, joined your ministry, and I'm not saying I regret that, I just . . . I just wish I could hear you once,
know that you feel the way that I know you — just a word. One
word. I know it's wrong to ask, but — Please. Tell me you're
with me. Tell me you're here. Please. God, my God, please, I'm
begging . . . talk to me. Please just talk to me.

Todd and Guy Go Camping
By Barbara Lindsay

Guy: thirties, is an all-American man's man male, the old-fashioned kind, not one of these New Age sensitive males. It takes the thought of impending death to break through the hearty testosterone show and reveal his loving heart.

Seriocomic

Best friends Todd and Guy have been camping in the desert. Their truck is broken, they are out of food and water, and they are lost. Guy believes they may not be rescued.

GUY: I gotta tell you something. It's personal, so listen. Just listen. Your Mustang? You know? That time? Right rear fender? Well. I did that. I didn't mean to, swear to God, but I . . . I . . . I drove it. No no no, I know, don't say anything, I know. I'm not finished, I still gotta tell you something. I gotta say it. OK. Just listen. Murray Cahill? We got stoned a coupla times and then told you we didn't. We told you there wasn't any. Three times. I mean, it was stupid, it was just Murray Cahill. I mean, who's Murray Cahill? He's nobody. It was just stupid and we were all stoned and all. But we did it. I thought you should know. And listen. Listen. Yeah. Well. There's something else. I gotta say it. Rhonda and me sometimes spend time together. We don't do anything, we never did anything. I swear to God that's true. We talk or walk or whatever. We never went to the movies, I swear to God. Nothing like that. I never put my hand under her bra. We never did, you know, anything. Nothing. We don't even talk about anything. We don't, you know, decide anything or, like, change each other's minds about anything. We drink coffee. I bought her an ice cream cone. One time. One stupid time. She, you know, she's where she wants to be. She doesn't want to be anywhere else. She loves you. She says that all the time. And Todd, I love you too, man. You're my . . . You're like my . . . You're like my soul mate. You know? You're my buddy. I got my life so mixed up in yours, it's like I don't even see it. You know? I dinged your Mustang, man. I'm sorry. And Murray Cahill is, you know, he was like a big goof, like who cares?

Marvel
By Joshua Scher

Sal: mid-thirties, a Caucasian, out-of-work window washer

Dramatic

> *Sal, dressed as Spider-Man, has climbed up a crane on the Brooklyn Bridge and is sitting on a platform hanging from it. Gabriella, an African-American N.Y. cop, still low on the totem pole, but high in idealism has been assigned to watch him nights. It is the second night and he is trying to make Gabriella understand why he is up there in protest. He has not seen his four-year-old daughter in over eight months.*

SPIDER-MAN: Why am I up here? Why do most people climb up a goddamn crane on the Brooklyn Bridge dressed as Spider-Man? *(Beat.)*

I dunno . . . to make people more aware, you know what I'm saying? About the situation with dads, like I was telling you. I mean, I don't think most people would be for dads not getting to see their kids. They just don't realize the system is, you know, biased that way. And I don't think that parents should be able to use their kids as ammo against each other. Shit, guess that's why they call it a nuclear family. I also figured . . . I know I can't get to see my little girl, but at least doing this, she gets to see me. Spider-Man is my daughter's favorite hero. I just — I know there's a lot of deadbeat dads out there who just shoot their rocks off and then shoot off and leave. I don't want her to ever think that was me, you know what I'm saying? That I didn't want to see her or be a part of her life. I don't want her to ever grow up angry at me. *(Beat.)*

I want her to grow up angry at her mother.

What He Can't Tell You
By Mark Loewenstern

Neil: thirties, scrappy, ambitious, macho

Dramatic

> *Neil has not told his materialistic girlfriend, Christine, that his business has failed, out of fear that she will leave him. But the pressures have gotten to him and Christine has just angrily confronted Neil on their waning sex life. This is his response.*

NEIL: You know, when I was fifteen, I wanted sex all the goddamn time. And if I was with a girl, and I wanted sex and she didn't, then *I* was the problem. And if I pushed her or pressured her, or asked her why we weren't having sex, then that made me an ogre. I was the bad, sex-crazed boy and I had to learn how to control myself. OK, fine. Now it's twenty years later, and I'm with you. And you want sex right now. Right now. And you're pushing, and you're mad because we're not having sex. And everything is reversed, except for one thing: I'm still the problem. Right? Because now I *don't* want it, that makes me the problem. So I guess — what? I guess I'm supposed to want it whenever you want me to want it. Right? Is that it? Is that the rule?

Untold Crimes of Insomniacs
By Janet Allard

The Cop: thirties, an officer of the law. He longs to believe that people can be good to one another.

Seriocomic

> When the married woman he is in love with shows up on his doorstep in the middle of the night, wanting his sympathy, The Cop tries to end his relationship with her once and for all.

THE COP: I know you want me to ask you in, Annie, because you are standing on my front stoop with a suitcase, but I'm not going to ask you in this time, Annie.

You know I get important calls in the middle of the night, Annie, I get calls where someone's just been shot — real emergencies, where people are dying here. Are you dying here? When the phone rings alarms go off, I am up and ready for action. This better not be a false alarm Annie. You're not here because you were dying to see me. You're here because you want me to save you. It's not about me Annie, it's about you.

You want to show up on my doorstep in the middle of the night and tell me about how your relationship is falling apart, and shower me with affection and butter me up and flirt and promise and flatter. I need someone who needs me 24-7. Not someone who wants me sometimes, needs me sometimes to put out a fire someone else started. I am not a fireman. I care, Annie, I care very much. And I feel like a real "bad guy" here for not letting you in — When I see that you are in a tight spot and you need a place to go — I hope you can forgive me, but I've made a decision, Annie and that decision is final. Sometimes there is an empty space within you and it feels like a black hole. But you need to go through that, Annie, you need to experience that empty place in order to allow something new to come into it. You need to create a vacuum to be filled. I need to start anew Annie. And so do you. OK? OK. OK?

Castles on the Coast of North Carolina
By John Michael Manship

Earl: mid-thirties, a conservative father

Dramatic

> *Rachel and Earl are siblings. Rachel cares very much for Earl's son, Daniel, but Earl doesn't want her near him. Here, Rachel has discovered that Daniel is having serious problems in school. She threatens Earl with contacting social services if he doesn't change his conservative methods of child rearing. Earl retorts.*

EARL: You want to *help?* Is that what you told them? And that ignorant man bought that load of crap? And then you tell me that this is about the *law?* This is about you and me and this is about you and Daddy. Don't lie to me. That's all you do is lie. You want to put *your* ideas into Daniel's head instead of mine. I can see right through you. You want me to believe that this is about the *law;* you can forget that. It's about brainwashing, and nobody's brainwashing my boy. The boy is too young for your crap. You're just the kind of person I'm trying to keep him away from. I'm his father. It's my decisions. People coming in here telling me I'm not doing my job right, well it's my fucking decisions. If I want to send him to Sunday School every day, it's my decision. If I want to teach him every Bible verse I know, that's my decision, too. I can send him to a private Christian institution — that's not *illegal* yet, is it? I don't care what they say. The Bible says, and Janet and I believe, that we know what's right for the boy, and you may have your ideas and think what I believe is backwater bullshit, but — I swear to God, Rachel, if you start using your *law* to try to get your ideas inside my boy's head . . . Come by for an honest visit sometime, you know?

The Good King
By John Shea

He: early thirties, husband, father of three, settled and happy, until news of his father's death forces him to see who he now is rather than who he was

Dramatic

As his father lies dying in a hospital bed on Christmas Eve, a man must come face-to-face with his past. He tries to rationalize his not wanting to go and say good-bye, while his wife tries to convince him that he should. The imminent death of his once abusive father forces He to confront his feelings and fears.

HE: *(Unable to joke.)* All he gave me is the ability to hate, and I hate that I can. But, hate is powerful, and for the first time in my life, I'm not afraid of him. He can't do anything to hurt me anymore. See, I do feel something. I'm not afraid. And I don't think it's just because he's dying. I'm not afraid because I hate him so much that I can't feel anything else. Not even fear. Maybe I should be grateful. He gave me the fear, now he's taking it away, only it's too late. He'll never know how I really feel . . .
(He turns, as if speaking to his father. He is angry, screaming, his words harsh, pointing a finger in what would be his father's face.)
   Shut up. You have nothing to say that I want to hear, so just shut up. You don't scare me. You want to threaten me, kill me? Go right ahead because I can't stop you, but I won't live in fear anymore. Look at you, you're a broken, lonely old man and when you die all you're going to leave behind is a bunch of terrified children who hate you but are too afraid to say so. Well, I'm not afraid anymore, so go ahead and have another heart attack, only this time make it a good one, so we can be done with you once and for all.
(Back to his old self, He turns to her, smiling, trying to hold back tears.)
   See? Tough, huh? Bet you didn't know I could be so tough.

The Pyre
By Terri Campion

Jeffrey: a struggling comedian in his thirties

Dramatic

Jeffrey testifies on behalf of his father who is dying of Mesothelioma, before a jury in a Class Action Suit against several Asbestos companies.

JEFFREY: What is a typical day for my father? Let's see. Mmmmm. Well, he gets up. Ooops! What am I thinking? That's me! My dad . . . he opens his eyes. If it's a good day we'll help him and his oxygen hose out of bed and we'll hobble across the hall to his den, where we'll sit him in his easy chair. He'll sit there and wait for my mother or his nurse to give him his meds. Then he'll nod off, coming out of his stupor when he's in pain and he'll moan and call out for my mother . . . or his momma. Visitors only agitate him. He'll tell you to go, or he'll ask you to help him die. He sees oil tankards and worries that he hasn't finished his job. Throughout the day my mother will feed him some jello or apple sauce. She and his nurse will clean his teeth and give him a sponge bath and maybe a shave if he isn't too ornery. On a good day he'll sit on the toilet to pee. Otherwise he goes in a bottle. Hasn't taken a dump in two weeks. There's nothing to dump. *(Pause.)* He'll look at you with terror and ask you questions. Questions that make no sense. Questions that indicate that he is in another living world where his mother and brothers are waiting for him in the kitchen. Where I'm a little boy with chicken pox. Where he is not this shell of a man sitting in a chair waiting for God to take him — but a vital healthy man, with plans for the day! And people that rely on him! That need him! Where he is walking around the oil refinery, surveying and estimating! That fucking oil refinery, for thirty-six years! Where every day for thirty-six years he was signing his own death warrant!

Ten Acrobats in an Amazing Leap of Faith
By Yussef El Guindi

Kamal: mid to late thirties

Dramatic

Kamal is having difficulty bringing up his Muslim children in the United States. He complains to his wife about the disrespectful and irreligious way in which one of his sons is behaving. His wife, Mona, is defending her children.

KAMAL: Being disrespectful and rude is growing up? Or is that what growing up means in this country? Treating your parents like they are something that has fallen out of fashion? Disposable. And while we're about it, let's throw God out too, because he doesn't go with all the latest trends and gadgets. He isn't cool enough. Isn't hip enough. He asks too much, demands too much; requires you to do too many things like give to the poor; be kind, fast so your mind may turn to him, pray so you may do the same and still the nonsense that goes on in your head; pray several times a day so when you talk with people you will remember him and not treat your fellows badly. That's all too much. Takes away from one's busy schedule of shopping and buying and watching TV, and everything else people begin to believe is essential to function — to be considered a healthy member of this society. *That's what being healthy means here.* And God has no place in it. — He's stored away until a crisis comes along. And then they take him out, dust him off, speak of him like he's the star player on the team they're on, ask of him miracles and when the crisis is over he's shoved off again; thank you very much, don't call us, we'll call you. This is the environment we brought Tawfiq up in . . . We should have stayed put and never have left our country!

A Bad Week for Therapy
By Barbara Lhota and Janet B. Milstein

Harry: thirties, a therapist

Comic

> *Martha has come to see Harry, a therapist, because she is having trouble in her work and personal life. Martha is incredibly timid and needs help gaining the self-confidence that will make her a more effective human being. Harry, unfortunately, has had a bad week . . . his girlfriend/ secretary left him, construction on his office building has begun, and his overbearing mother has dropped in unexpectedly. As this monologue begins, Harry is trying to fill out standard forms with Martha.*

HARRY: I used to have a secretary who did this. She quit Monday out of the blue. With no warning, leaving me high and dry. My files were a mess, my life was even . . . ! Anyway, not that I should be telling you this, Martha. Who wants an angry therapist, huh? Not that I'm angry. I'm not angry. Actually very calm and collected, usually, but when your . . . secretary up and leaves, well . . . ! *(Furious.)* Ten years we were together! *(Claps his hand.)* 5, 4, 3, 2, 1. *(He inhales deeply and then exhales. To Martha.)* It's a little tough around here right now. Course them deciding to reconstruct the whole building out of nowhere last week . . . No warning! Not a bit of warning. That made things a little challenging. And then of course, my overbearing mother decides to drop by from Pittsburgh and I just want to slam her face into the . . . *(Exhales sharply.)* Just a bad week. OK, um, welcome, Martha. I'm so glad you're here. I just want to say that I like to create in my office a warm and pleasant and safe environment for you so that you can explore — do you hear that banging? *(Calling to the ceiling.)* Shut up!! I'm trying to work down here! *(To Martha. Smiles.)* It feels good to get help, doesn't it? *(Noticing her expression.)* Oh gosh. Did I scare you, Martha? I'm sorry. I apologize. Things aren't generally so tense. It was just the abruptness of everything that threw me really. It's not like I ever intended for us to become . . . Well, *(Laughs.)* I seem to be a bit distracted. I'm, I'm not usually distracted like this. OK, so um, so . . . um . . . You just want a little kindness — a little sympathy when things end. *(Wallowing in the moment, shaking out of it.)* OK. *(Claps.)* OK now. Um, let's not focus on me here. My focus is you. This is for you. This session is about you. Uh, let's talk about *you*.

Management Orientation
By Adam Simon

Adams: thirties, bigwig of a pharmaceutical company, self-assured, off-kilter

Dramatic

> *On a conference call with his staff, Adams angrily debates the merits of releasing a new AIDS drug that guarantees five more years of life but then also guarantees death at the end of that time. While the two employees are in the conference room, Adams is on speakerphone. Even though Adams claims to be in Africa, he is actually in another room on the floor and watching on a monitor as the lower level managers write illicit things on the dry erase board, eat, and sarcastically gesture at what Adams says. Finally Adams enters the scene, surprising the underlings and lets them have it.*

ADAMS: You think I'd let anything go on here of even the most minor significance without seeing it? You think I don't know that Williams here masturbates in the fifth-floor bathroom every day between 2:15 and 2:30? You think I don't know that you look at Internet porn with regularity, your favorite target being young Russian tennis starlets? You think that everything escapes me don't you?! Well you're wrong. Nothing escapes me. I can tell you the color of the receptionist's shit and the days that my administrative assistant is on her period. I could tell you things about some of the people here that would make your stomach turn and force the food to come spewing out of your throat, at least that's what it did to me when I first started finding these things out. No less than four convicted sex offenders work here, did you know that?

Management Orientation
By Adam Simon

Adams: thirties, bigwig of a pharmaceutical company, self-assured, off-kilter

Dramatic

> *On a conference call with his staff, Adams angrily debates the merits of releasing a new AIDS drug that guarantees five more years of life but then also guarantees death at the end of that time.*

ADAMS: You're telling me that we're going to make this drug that will keep people with AIDS alive for five more years than they could otherwise live and then kill them? You're telling me that you could sleep at night knowing that all you've effectively done is increased the number of people with AIDS? Do you think that people are going to spend their newfound five years celibate as a monk? No, they're going to screw like mad and all that means is more of an epidemic. And contrary to what some people around here might think, that is not good for business.

Traces
By Charles Evered

Norman: thirties, a homeless man on the run from the Mob

Dramatic

Norman explains his predicament to Helen, a woman sheltering him from the bad guys.

NORMAN: Hey, listen to me, alright? I remember a time, believe it or not, but I remember a time when I would walk by guys that I look like now, on the street, and I used to say to myself, "heck with them," ya know? Like I was pissed at them for not doin' what I thought was their job to do. You know, just take care of themselves, and to get their own crap together, and to get their hands out of my face every time I walked by 'em. And then, after what *seemed* like little thing after little thing started happening to me. After I lost *my* job, and *my* wife and *my* kids, and I started realizing that sooner or later I'd be losin' the house that I was losin' everything in — well, then I started feeling a little less high and mighty to 'em, ya know? All those hands in my face when I would walk by 'em on my way to Arby's, where I was working for some eighteen-year-old pimply high school kid for four twenty-five an hour. So don't tell me how I feel about myself, if you don't know what you're talkin' about — that OK with you?

If Only
By Barbara Lhota and Janet B. Milstein

Rob: thirty-five years old, Shannon's husband

Dramatic

> *Rob's wife, Shannon, got into a collision with an SUV. Both she and their ten-year-old son, Michael, were critically injured. This morning Rob had the painful task of explaining the extent of their son's injuries to his wife. Because there has been some additional controversy about the car accident, including some questions about Shannon's alcohol level, she has been very critical about how Rob handled things. In this speech, Rob urges Shannon to see how difficult things have been for him too.*

ROB: I know this is hard for you. I know that! But will you just think of *my* side of things for once?! I've been pacing the halls in this God-forsaken hospital for the last two days, praying you'd be alive. I haven't eaten. I haven't slept. I just wander from room to room asking for more reports about you and Michael. More reports from doctors who just don't know anything. *I've* been furious too. I totally lost it yesterday with some doctor for not doing things fast enough. Furious with all the people asking questions — the police, the insurance company, friends. A million forms to fill out and a million people that I don't know how to deal with. I'm holding your hand for hours while people come in and out acting as if I've already lost you. I want to throw furniture out the window. My whole life has changed in an instant. I don't know if I'm alone in the world. Do you know how that feels? I don't know if my son will ever walk or be able to live with me. I don't know whose fault it is. I should have been with you instead of working on a Saturday. And you shouldn't have driven in that damn weather when you were . . . I didn't mean . . . It's just . . . I hear the "if-onlys" in my head too. And all you can do is tell me what I haven't done. What I should have done. Well . . . what about *you?*

Moving Picture
By Dan O'Brien

Willie Dickson: thirty-four

Dramatic

> *Willie Dickson has found out that he's been betrayed by his mentor, Thomas Edison. This is the day that Dickson confronts him, and the day he quits and says good-bye to Edison forever.*

DICKSON: What happened to make you like this? Did your mother not love you? Did no one love you? Did you even have a mother, or were you self-begotten? You're just a man . . . You're arrogant, you're conniving, you're crass, your jokes aren't even remotely funny. You're not smart — I mean real intelligence, human imagination and empathy. You've got no idea what it's like to be anyone other than yourself. You're not a god — .

    The people who work for you despise you. Your enemies wish you would get sick and die, even your so-called friends are really just afraid of you. Your children hate you and your wife died alone. — You'll die alone too if you don't watch yourself.

I-2195
By Barbara Lindsay

Rex: thirties, is a hot-blooded, hot-tempered survivalist, always itch-
ing for a fight, impulsive, roaringly manly. He leaves the politics
of their cause to Lucinda. For him, she is the only thing in life
worth fighting for.

Dramatic

*Rex Eaglejeep and Lucinda Celest are former freedom fight-
ers, now in hiding. Rex is urging Lucinda to take up the
fight again.*

REX: To say you don't want to fight any more is like a drowning man
saying he doesn't want to swim any more. Jesus H. Christ on a
fucking rotisserie spit, Lucinda, what's wrong with you? I know
you got used to thinking you're all alone, living up here in the
woods away from everything, but I'm telling you, girl chick, the
public battery is charged. Anybody so much as whispers your
name, we got a march on our hands. Maybe it starts off as nos-
talgia, but pretty soon it's an oiled machine of one thousand and
one moving parts. And goddamn it, Lucinda, you don't count
victories and losses and the dead. You just go forward and you
be who you need to be. Are you fading on me? Do you want to
run instead of fight? Tell me. I lay no judgment. Tell me if you
want to run. We could do that. We could go and start over someplace else, and this time find a place that's prettier or more fruit-
ful, and maybe have five whole years before they find us and
hound us and take everything away. Do you think I don't see the
appeal in that? Do you think I don't want to live out my days in
peace with you? But we'd be two corpses, girl chick, and you
know it. There'd be nothing left but the meat package. How it
all got to where it is today is too many people turned themselves
into corpses instead of putting up a fight. I'm not fighting for
dirt and boundaries here. I'm not fighting for the sheer joy of it,
although there's plenty of that, don't get me wrong. But there
have to be those who fight. We're the ones who keep the shape
of the whole, because we keep carving away at it, carving away.

Aunt Raini
By Tom Smith

Joel: early thirties, a Jewish photographer

Dramatic

> *Joel, in his thirties, is a Jewish photographer. While brows-*
> *ing through some books of his longtime girlfriend, Kather-*
> *ine, he comes across a book about the official*
> *documentarian of the Third Reich. He looks at the dust*
> *jacket and realizes the documentarian is Katherine's aunt,*
> *Raini, who is visiting from Germany. Before he can confront*
> *Katherine and Raini with his discovery, Raini suffers a mas-*
> *sive heart attack and dies. A few days later, Joel tries to con-*
> *vince Katherine to destroy the Nazi films her aunt*
> *bequeathed her.*

JOEL: Katie, I liked your Aunt Raini. She was smart, she was funny, she told it like it was. But I'll be honest with you — when I saw her picture on that dust jacket . . . when I realized she was the same person who aided the Third Reich — Katie, I wished her dead. I did. I know that sounds harsh, but I sat there and wished she were dead! *(Beat.)*

The only way not to repeat history is to understand it. I'm telling you this because I want you to understand how many thousands — millions — of people's lives your aunt destroyed through her films. Even if she didn't mean for it to happen, she contributed to all that . . . horror. That bloodstain on the fabric of history. And you wouldn't be so pissed off at me if you didn't think that what I'm saying is true. *(Pause.)*

You have to help ease the pain of the past. You have that responsibility now. You've got to destroy those originals of her films, Katie! *(Beat.)*

Because they're powerful enough to inspire someone else to become the next Hitler.

Good News
By Joshua Scher

Marco: thirty, a young screenwriter

Comic

> *The Writer's Room, in a world where the New Testament never existed; Marco has sold his first screenplay (which is essentially the Christ story). The only hitch is he must work with Matt, Luca, and Johnny to rewrite the script and present it by tomorrow's deadline. He has reached a breaking point, as the other three have argued back and forth about how to "fix" his story. Frustrated and desperate, Marco offers a new solution that will make everyone happy.*

MARCO: We can give them something else, write something else. They'll never know. Same time period. Same characters. Completely different story. No son of God. No miracles. No metaphysical meaning. How about just some fishermen and their sea in good ol' Galilee? And maybe throw in some muscle men goring each other in a coliseum. Hunh, how 'bout it? *The Perfect Storm* meets *Spartacus?* That's what they want anyway. They don't want my story. They told me they don't want my story. They said so. That's why the three of you are here. We'll just write them an entirely new story. Won't that be fun? You guys can do it. All of you. You are so talented and good-looking. I'll stay out. Just let me have it back and you'll never hear from me or my script again. OK? Great. *(Beat.)* Please? Please? *(Pause.)*
    Fuck you all. You parasites. You hacks. You tail riders. I hope you choke on a phone book.

Stuck Outside of Dayton with the Bob Dylan Blues Again
By Dennis Schebetta

Tweedy: late twenties to thirties, a musician in a Bob Dylan tribute band.

Seriocomic

> *Tweedy and Deegan are stuck on the side of the road, stuck in their friendship, and stuck in their musical careers. Seems that a Bob Dylan tribute band is a hard sell. And when Deegan learns of Tweedy's infidelity with his girlfriend a few years ago, he decides to quit. But Tweedy convinces him not to give it all up.*

TWEEDY: That's bullshit! You can't give up your dreams, man! What we got is bigger than you and Jenny and you and me and everything. God, man, could you ever forget that feeling we had our first gig at The Living Room? Both of us, nervous as shit, hands shaking, throat dry, and even though we rehearsed for months we still didn't feel ready. All our friends and family were out there anticipating our great debut. I didn't think I'd even have a voice but when I started singing the first song, oh man —
(Sings.)
    "She's got everything she needs, she's an artist, she don't look back."
(Speaks again.)
    Suddenly the whole bar went silent. Not even the sound of clinking glasses. And I know you wanted to open with "Tangled Up in Blue" — same argument we've had for years. But the song didn't matter — we grabbed them because of our passion, our intensity, and our commitment to play one honest note. And now every time we play together, all those petty arguments in the van over which album is better "Blonde on Blonde" or "Blood on the Tracks" and all that unnecessary bullshit just fades away and what's left is that connection. You're turning your back on

me, sure, but if you leave now you're turning your back on that, too. So OK, you're pissed about Johanna — hell, I'd be pissed, too — and if you never want to speak to me again, that's fine, dude, whatever. But you're killing something else here. More than just a friendship. And you know it.

Games
By Jeannine Coulombe

Tony: early to mid-thirties

Dramatic

> *Kept from contact with his now three-year-old son, Tony*
> *confronts his ex-wife, who is about to remarry, and tries to*
> *convince her to allow some thread to exist between himself*
> *and his son.*

TONY: No, wait. Please. Don't close the door. Please. Is he there?
Wait. I'm not leaving. You can shut me out of *your* life, but you
can't shut me out of *his*. He's my son. No matter how much you
wish he wasn't, he is. You can't change that. No matter how
much you try. He's half me as much as he's half you. Marrying
this guy doesn't give Jake a father because he already has one.
I'm right here. Wait. Please. I'm his father. I should have some
right to say what I need to say. It doesn't matter what happened
between us. Be mad at me. Be mad, I don't care. But please don't
let his life go by without me in it. He doesn't even know me.
Goddamn it. No, wait. I never wanted this to happen. Don't let
this happen. Please. Look at me. I'm shaking just knowing he's
behind that door. I'm so close to him and yet I . . . goddamn it.
He doesn't even know who I am. And I should know him. He's
my son. So . . . look . . . maybe you can't let me in right now.
OK. I don't have to meet him right now. Maybe we're not ready
for that. But . . . but, I don't want him going to bed every night
thinking his father doesn't care. Even if he has some other guy
there. He should at least know my voice. Can we start with that?
Please. I bought this book. See? And uhmm . . . it was one I had
when I was a kid and . . . I made this CD with me reading it,
OK? So he can hear my voice. That's all I'm asking. Just do this
one thing. Please?

Marvel
By Joshua Scher

Sal: mid-thirties, a Caucasian, out-of-work window washer

Dramatic

Sal, dressed as Spider-Man, has climbed up a crane on the Brooklyn Bridge and is sitting on a platform hanging from it in order to protest for fathers' rights. He has not seen his four-year-old daughter in over eight months. Gabriella, an African-American N.Y. cop, still low on the totem pole, but high in idealism has been assigned to watch him nights. It is the sixth night, almost dawn, Sal has promised Gabriella he would come down before sunrise. But he has changed the plan.

SAL: The insurance won't pay if it's a suicide. I told you that. I told you window washers get good benefits. You said it yourself the other night. Do the most amount of good available to you and shit. Try something else. Four million is a lot of good, don't you think? Abi would be set for life. It's more than I could ever provide. She could do whatever she wants. For all I know, Livi told her I'm dead already. *(Beat.)*

Don't you get it? It's true. I am dead. They're going to Minnesota, I can't follow, I can't stop them, I can't do shit! I can't even do this on my own. I've got nothing. Nothing to offer her. Except four million dollars. And I'll be damned if you're going to stop me from giving it to her. *(Beat.)*

Shit, I didn't plan this. I didn't plan Minnesota. And it doesn't matter what was planned or not. What matters is what works. *(Beat.)*

Look you don't have to kill me or nothing. You could just wing me. Give me a reason to fall off and into the river. I'll take care of the rest. You wouldn't be killing me. You'd be assisting me, like that doctor. Delorean. Just so it doesn't look like a suicide.

Dangerous
By Tom Smith

Marcus: early thirties, a wealthy and vindictive playboy

Dramatic

> *In this modern-day, all-male retelling of* Les Liaisons Dangereuses, *Marcus, in his early thirties, persuades his friend Alexander to seduce the new boyfriend of Grayson, Marcus's ex-lover, in revenge of their breakup.*

MARCUS: We all have gifts, Alexander, and mine happens to be the gift of observation. I noticed the quick turning off of the computer when I entered the room, the increased amount of time spent at the gym with little results, and, most incriminatingly, the credit card receipts with charges that were not incurred on business dinners. It's almost insulting how stupid Grayson must think I am. The flirtation has been going on for two weeks, but they landed the deal, so to speak, Thursday evening in the young lad's apartment. Poor boy was more inexperienced than Grayson anticipated: just adolescent groping in the dark. It seems he's waiting to give himself completely, as it were, until he finds true love. Which is why I intended to give you a call this evening. I want you to not only beat Grayson to the punch, but do it in such a public manner that he'll be humiliated. I'd do it myself, but it would seem so vindictive. But you, if you were to do it . . . well, it would just be another conquest for you. Grayson would find himself breaking up with the boy before they're even officially dating. Then, as he showers me with affection to ease his guilty remorse, I shall very publicly rebuke him, thus ensuring he pays for his crime with his dignity. He'll be cuckolded, and no one goes near a fool, save another fool. So . . . ? Will you do it?

Ten Acrobats in an Amazing Leap of Faith
By Yussef El Guindi

Aziz: Wise, tolerant, with a good sense of humor, mid-thirties to fifties

Seriocomic

> *Aziz and Tawfiq are arguing about God. Aziz, a Sufi, is trying to stay open to Tawfiq's aggressive, atheistic stance. Aziz's first line is a response to Tawfiq's outburst about why — "if God is a language no one can speak properly — why can't people just stop talking about God."*

AZIZ: And yet people cannot. We cannot seem to shut up about God. Anywhere. Is that not a puzzle in itself? We chatter on about him like fools. Like the weak people we are, going on about someone we cannot finally prove. I cannot prove anything to you about him. The evidence I would show you that he exists would be the same evidence you would show me to prove that he doesn't exist. I would say, "here we are, isn't that proof enough." And you would say, "yes, here we are. There is no evidence of anything else." — And your argument should win the day. It should, really. Maybe God is something that happened to people long ago because they didn't have television. Something to amuse themselves in the desert, and God is a pretty good story, so why not. And yet — people still do not let go. Is it a weakness? That should crumble with the first good scientific explanation? — And yet it does not. We should have come to the conclusion by now that he's not there. But so many continue with this fairy tale because we find nothing to explain this thing inside us that says, *this is not all there is* . . . And not all the hard facts and knowledge of science could ever satisfy this longing. And to live that longing with all the faith and passion we have. And if not believing in God gives you the same excitement, then, maybe, you and I can end up believing in the same thing. — That we don't know enough to ever close our eyes to anything. And maybe in that way, we both move forward as believers . . . Yes?

Out of Place
By David Robson

Danny Dagan: thirties, Israeli police officer

Dramatic

> *Danny is a former American now living in Israel and working as a police officer. He's speaking to Edmund Hassan, a noted Palestinian-American scholar who, after being arrested on suspicion of terrorism, is now questioning his identity and beliefs. Here Danny reveals to Edmund his own crisis of faith and how he discovered who he really was.*

DANNY: I was raised Catholic. Back in '83 I came with the church — we visited a Kibbutz — had a chance to work with my hands for the first time in my life, growing corn, building houses. Even had my first taste of matzo ball soup. It opened me up in ways my own faith never had. Don't know what it was. It was simpler somehow, and truer. I never liked all that pomp and circumstance. Then five years ago I converted. My parents weren't too happy about it; they didn't get it. For them a world without Jesus Christ is like a world without Republicans. For me, it was like when you hear about someone wanting to change his sex. The guy never says, "I wanted to be a woman." He says, "I always *was* a woman. I just didn't have the right equipment." The way I look at it I was born a Jew. But for thirty some-odd years I just never had the right equipment. And I figured what better way to support the state of Israel than to live here.

Some Place on the Road . . .
By Julius Galacki

Poetry Salesman: mid-twenties to mid-thirties. He is a man of nearly undefeatable enthusiasm. He literally cannot stop selling. He's also filled with a literal, unquenchable hunger.

Comic

> *Previous to this scene, the Salesman has ordered a "Carnivore Special No. 1" at the worst diner in the world, but he has only been served inedible burnt toast — twice. After one last temptation that his meat will finally be served, the Waitress confronts "Mr. Sophisticated Traveling Salesman" with the fact that she doubts he has any money. Unfortunately, he sells poetry anthologies that just aren't an in-demand product. If the Salesman had any awareness, he would know, as he finally does at the end of the play, that he has already starved to death and is now in Purgatory.*

SALESMAN: You want to humiliate me. Saying I don't have the money to pay you for a Carnivore Special No. 1. But let me tell you . . . I want to tell you . . . No. No. I can't pretend anymore. You saw through me the moment I walked in the door. It's all true. I am broke. But I don't want you to forget something. You said, you're feeling trapped here. And no matter what a liar I am, it doesn't change the fact that the greatest truths are right here in this suitcase. I have your answer to happiness. You begin with the Word and end with the Word. In between you fly, fly, fly, far away from here. What do you think poetry really is? It's Harrison Ford in *The Fugitive*. It's uh . . . uh . . . why do you think, back in Communist Russia, people died to hear a good poem!?

Management Orientation
By Adam Simon

Adams: thirties, bigwig of a pharmaceutical company, self-assured, off-kilter

Seriocomic

> *On a conference call with his staff, Adams angrily debates the merits of releasing a new AIDS drug that guarantees five more years of life but then also guarantees death at the end of that time. At this point he is describing his new African bride whom he found in a catalogue of wives and then fell in love with.*

ADAMS: So anyway, that's what I'm thinking about when I land on this little tiny airstrip (after making my connection) in the middle of nowhere. And you know what I find out about my bride to be? First off, she's just as beautiful as I had thought and secondly I find out (through my interpreter of course) that Yatima isn't her real birth name. When she was born her parents named her Myeisha which means "one who is loved greatly." And then her parents both die of AIDS after one of them (nobody knows which) cheats on the other one and now everybody calls her Yatima which means "orphan." If that doesn't turn you around, nothing will. So I hope this explains why I'm not about to put out some drug that turns a whole lot of Myeisha's into a bunch of Yatima's.

The Cowboy Who Used a Dally Rope
By Dylan Guy

Reynolds: thirty-eight, guilt-ridden, tormented, his defenses down

Dramatic

> *After the funeral of their father, Reynolds, a young ordained priest, goes to the family cabin in upstate New York. He is carrying a terrible secret. His younger brother, Clarence, suspects the truth and follows him to the cabin. While there, Clarence succeeds in breaking through to his brother so that Reynolds can confess the truth.*

REYNOLDS: I just did what I thought was best. The old man was sick. He wasn't ever going to get well. Watching him day after day hooked up to those machines, knowing it was no use. And then, on that day, it rained. You know how he always hated the rain. It rained on that day. It rained for hours. I went into his room and he was sleeping. I remember wondering if it was raining in his sleep. He always used to say he wanted to go in his sleep. Remember? He used to say that? He used to say he wanted to go when he was peaceful. That day, he was peaceful. Somebody had to do something. Somebody had to, didn't they? Everything has always been left up to me. Ever since I can remember. You were the younger, it's always been left to me. God forgive me. I just wish I knew if it was raining in his sleep.

Shining Sea
By Jonathan Dorf

Candy: in his mid-thirties, homeless homeless, car-window squeegee
man and the kind of guy who is always working some angle

Dramatic

> *Candy, mid-thirties, is a squeegee man living in New York
> City, but the New York in which he lives is one in which
> there are now two rival Mayors, and the city is falling into
> chaos and civil war. He has been savagely beaten by a park-
> ing authority goon squad, the word* violation *imprinted on
> his body, and he recounts to Violet, forty-something woman
> and part of his squeegee family, what has happened and how
> he was saved.*

CANDY: They made me run alongside the tow truck. Until out of
nowhere they stop and say I can go. "You're lucky we got
another one, Violation." *(Beat.)*
　　It was a kid. Not a kid like Pac's a kid, but a little kid. Little kid on a scooter. They stop right in front of him, and before
he can go around, one of 'em says he wants the scooter for *his*
kid. The kid sees he can't run, so he gives 'em the scooter. Just
picks it up and hands it to 'em. One of 'em slings it into the cab
of the truck, and the other one asks the kid if he'd like to try driving. Least they can do for taking his scooter, he says. The kid
says OK, like maybe he's thinking if he talks to them, it won't be
that bad. Talk his way out of it. But when the kid turns to get in,
they grab him. He sort of kicks and screams for a second, and
then he just goes limp. Not limp — calm. The kid lets them hook
him up to the harness, and when they get back inside the cab,
just between when they put it in gear and when they start moving, he looks at me. *(Beat.)*
　　I'm hidin' in a doorway, but he knows that. He's known that
the whole time and he just looks at me real peaceful, like he
knows — twelve-year-old kid, thirteen-year-old kid — he knows
it's not a good time to be alive. Stay in that doorway, save yourself — there's nothing for me here. That's what his eyes said.
Then the truck pulls away, and from the looks of it, he's dead in
half a block.

Shining Sea
By Jonathan Dorf

Candy: in his mid-thirties, homeless car-window squeegee man and
    the kind of guy who is always working some angle

Seriocomic

> *Candy, mid-thirties, is a squeegee man living in New York*
> *City, but the New York in which he lives is one in which*
> *there are now two rival Mayors, and the city is falling into*
> *chaos and civil war. He talks to Violet and Pac, his "fami-*
> *ly," a forty-something woman and a young man, nineteen,*
> *respectively, as he explains his current uneasiness with the*
> *escalating unrest.*

CANDY: *(There's a car alarm sound.)* When I was little, my Pops
    would make me go to bed at eight — we're talkin' when I was
    six, maybe seven — and as soon as I'd turn out the lights, he'd
    start mowin' the lawn. Crank up the floodlights and cart out the
    oldest working lawn mower in the history of the world. Needed
    a paint job, needed an oiling, needed a muffler in the worst way.
    Three times a week, eight o'clock: mow the lawn. Neighbors
    didn't mind too much in the summer — half of them were at the
    shore — but every other time of the year it was World War III.
    I'd stay up half the night, couldn't get the damn lawn mower
    sound outta my head. Or I'd stay up listening to the people:
    them complaining at him, him screaming at them, them calling
    the cops, him screaming at the cops, the cops haulin' him off to
    cool down. Even on the nights he didn't mow, I'd still stay up,
    waiting for the sound — *(There's the pop of gunfire, again from*
    about where the car alarm sound came.)
        And then I start to sleep through it. I sleep through the mow-
    ing and the screaming and the sirens. Regular little log. Wake up
    from yet another good night's sleep at the age of nine to find my
    Mom crying louder than a tribe of monkeys and my Pops a for-
    mer person. I use both hands to pull the knife out of his chest,
    then go back upstairs to squeeze in another hour. By the time I

wake up, my Mom is gone and the cops are there, and I'm sleepin' like the dead for the next thirty years. *(Beat.)*

Now I hear those guns in the street, that pop pop pop — it's starting to mess with my sleep again.

Into the Wind
By Adrienne Perry

Randy Dreyfus: late thirties, once a decorated police detective, now he's at the end of his rope mentally and professionally

Dramatic

> *Dreyfus is interrogating the mother of a murdered six-year-old girl. Grace Temple has been amazingly unhelpful and quiet in discussing anything to do with her daughter Samantha. Dreyfus is suffering under the load of past failures, himself. He knows he has to break Grace in order to solve the case and move on in his own life.*

DREYFUS: Grace, if there's someone else we need to know. You know what we've been thinking . . . when there's no other evidence, children of Sammy's age, the statistics show that it's usually the parents. Do you want us to think that? Talk to me.

I know what this feels like, damn it! One thing we're never supposed to do is get attached. Do you understand? I've been there, Grace. Lost someone.

Do you know who Christy Hazleton was? About six years ago, I was assigned to a case specifically to protect her. Nut case was going around stalking models based out of the West Coast. Her name turned up on his list. Stepanski's.

I got the collar. That was my job. But God help me, I fell in love with her, and that wasn't. After she died . . . I am guilty. By omission. I didn't tell her that *he* knew. Stepanski knew. You think you're the only ones who've been in the tabloids? The last time I saw her, I escorted her to his sentencing. The photographers were there in droves. There was a picture of me and . . . A year ago, he sent it to me. After he killed her. He sat on it that long, until his case was overturned on some damn technicality.

Grace, sometimes it's just your gut instinct. Criminals aren't just convicted on evidence. Sometimes we can see inside them, predict their behavior. The minute I saw that picture in the *Star,* I could see what a lovesick fool I was. And I should have known that he'd see it and act on it if he got the chance. But instead I panicked. I kept away from her. Pretended that she didn't matter to me. If only I had told her . . . Come on Grace, don't do what I did. Don't hold back. Tell me. Please.

Christy would be alive if it weren't for my silence.

The Last Stand of the Comanche Rider
By Elise Forier

Palmer Reese: thirties, former rodeo trick rider, in and out of jail
since he was nineteen for a variety of violent crimes including
armed robbery

Dramatic

> *Northeastern Arizona. The present. A tragic incident in*
> *Palmer's past — his drug-addled mother lighting their home*
> *on fire, killing herself and nearly killing Palmer, his stepsis-*
> *ter Josie and his half brother Calvin — has left him unable*
> *to connect with other people. Calvin, a half-breed Navajo,*
> *has been mixed up in a racial dispute with a neo-Nazi skin-*
> *head, who has subsequently been found murdered in a gully*
> *nearby. Palmer is speaking to Michaelene Rhyner, an older*
> *woman who has been caring for Calvin, and who believes*
> *him innocent of the murder. Calvin's epilepsy causes him to*
> *have visions, which Michaelene believes are divinely*
> *inspired.*

PALMER: He has temporal lobe epilepsy for Christ's sake! He has bad
wiring in his head. That's it . . . Let me tell you something, you
don't know what a person can do. No matter how sweet they
seem. But Josie here can tell you. Was Mama sweet, Josie? Sure
she was. She used to cut angels out of old Christmas cards and
hang them around the house. She'd come out to the riding circle
when we were practicing, bringing glasses of lemonade and
chocolate chip cookies, right? That woman could kiss you good
night and you'd swear to God no real person could smell that
good. And then one night, she just took a — she took a match
and blew everything from fucking here to kingdom come. You
think he hears angels? You think it's really God talking to him in
his head? Let me tell you something lady, he doesn't have a goddamn thing in his head. I was wearing steel toed boots the night
of the fire. He was lying right in front of the door, passed out
from smoke and heat and when I come in to see what's happening. I pulled the door open and I kicked him so hard in the head

his ears bled. That's what made him what he is! Not God! Not God! I kicked him . . . and he's never . . . he's never . . . Calvin, for Christ's sake stop looking at me. I'm sorry. I'm sorry I hurt you so bad.

Strangers in Lamaze
By Mark W. Cornell

Phil: early thirties, a wry, but bitter policeman who has fallen into despair over a series of personal failures

Seriocomic

> *Phil and Holly are an unhappily married couple expecting their first child. The baby, however, is not Phil's. He is impotent. And Holly has gone to a sperm donor. Arriving early to Lamaze class, Holly admits that Phil's growing bitterness has made him seem a stranger to her. Here Phil expresses deep frustrations and how he, too, feels like a stranger — to himself.*

PHIL: You know, you get it in your mind how you want your life to go. You get this picture. Some dream. And you work for that, you live for that. And then it doesn't turn out that way. The picture gets distorted. What is this thing we're living then? It's unnatural, unreal. *(Beat.)* All I've wanted was a nice little house, a comfortable amount of money, and a career as a detective. I had hopes. But it just didn't work out. We have a dumpy little apartment, no money, and I'm not a detective. I've worked every position at that police station except for the one I want. Now I'm the death messenger. It's just agonizing calling people and telling them that their brother died in a car accident, or their father was shot, or their kid drowned in the river. And it's even worse in person. I have to look at them. It's horrible. And now, people know my face. They're terrified of me. I went for a walk in the park last Sunday, you should have seen the people scatter. You'd have thought a tiger was running loose. *(Beat.)* Holly, you don't know what I've been through. I've lost sight of things . . . of me. I don't recognize anything. My job . . . my apartment . . . you . . . and now this child. It's not mine. I'm not going to recognize it. This wasn't how my life was supposed to be. I am a stranger, Holly. To you and to me.

The Hope Campaign
By Erica Rosbe

Wilco: twenties to thirties, a mounted policeman

Seriocomic

> *Wilco, a mounted policeman, has recently woken up from a coma after having been shot by a delusional girl scout. He's recently gathered the courage to rejoin the force, but he is having trouble keeping calm. Here, Wilco has returned to the coma ward after a traumatic experience to seek solace from the nurse, Mabel, with whom he is falling in love.*

WILCO: There was a girl-scout convention in the Park and I was the only mounted policeman on duty so I tried to stay calm. Dug my heels into my stirrups. But there was a sea of them, all green and brown, wearing those Hitler Jugend sashes. And that song, that Venice Blue song about the . . . the . . . you know . . . it started to play in my head, telling me *I* was a rapist — Then they all started to look at me, with their tiny, judging eyes. They said, you did this to us, evil MAN. They all started to walk toward me, smiling razors of crooked baby teeth . . . Cookies! Did I want to buy some cookies? They held out their green and gold boxes of Arsenic Delights and Rat Poison Mints at me and their sharp little paws were grabbing at me and it was then that I saw their guns — So I kicked Chester. I kicked him hard — too hard and I screamed, "I DID NOT RAPE YOU AND I WILL NOT BUY YOUR COOKIES" And he reared and they all jumped back and some of them started to cry I think and they parted as Chester and I galloped to the edge of the park . . . away from the screams of "Daddy!" and "My Caramel Delights!" across Woodward, toward the stadium and . . . I heard *your* voice in my head, the wake up, and I said of course, "wake up, Wilco" this is all some bad dream and your voice was overpowering the Venice song, like Wonder Woman killing . . . whoever it was that was her enemy . . . and I had to see you, had to hear you, Mabel, because it wasn't a dream, it was real and all I wanted to do was to be under you hearing you whisper "wake up." That was the safest place I could think of. The warmest place.

System Eternal
By Chance D. Muehleck

George Enemy: mid-thirties, a large man who's been in and out of prison most of his life

Dramatic

> *George's sister Catherine is dead, and George thinks he's killed her in a blackout. His best friend Wally tries to convince him otherwise, but with little evidence. Here, George tells Wally why he should turn himself in.*

GEORGE: I wanna thank you, man. You're a prick sometimes. But thanks. You always looked after me. That goes a long way. But I'm at the stop of this fuckin' road. All the mad I get. All the dumb stupid mad. I'm like a monster. Like one of those village monsters people torch. I walk around on my big dumb feet. What am I waiting for? This was gonna happen. I smote her, Wally. My poor sweet sister. I laid her out. *(Pause.)*

There's good in me, right? I mean, I have a good side. A nice side. A go-to-the-grocery-and-pick-up-the-milk side. It's big, too. That side is big. But you know what? I got a bad side. And the bad is stronger. Its colors run deep. And every day it gets painted on by common things. Little things. The good is big, but it's got fuzzy edges. You know? There's nothin' for it to grip onto. Bad don't even have to look; colors just come into it. Bad knows what it wants. Good is a puppy. A big dumb puppy. And by the time it sees Bad leading it by the nose, it's too late. The damage is done. *(Pause.)*

I don't even get to bury her.

Don't Dance Me Outside
By William Borden

Butch: thirty to sixty, a moderately successful novelist

Dramatic

> *Butch and Ardis, both married, have just begun an affair.*
> *They've spent the past several hours in a hotel room making*
> *love, getting to know each other, making love some more,*
> *and getting to know each other better. Now Ardis has*
> *revealed an episode from her past that explains an inner*
> *truth about herself. Butch is moved to reveal his own*
> *inner truth.*

BUTCH: I saw a woman murdered the other day. Coming out of her
apartment building. She was about my age. She had red hair. She
was wearing a black dress and dark glasses. She was putting her
keys in her purse. She didn't look worried. Maybe she was thinking, I'll go to the grocery, then I'll pick up some lunch. Her purse
was still open, and this guy climbed out of his car, and he yelled
at her, "Bitch! I saw who you was with last night!" — something
like that, and he pulled out a pistol, and she didn't even look sur-
prised, or maybe she didn't see the gun, or she didn't believe
it — and he shot her, three, maybe four, times. She fell down the
steps. The stuff in her purse spilled all over. He looked at her a
few seconds, then he got in the car and drove off. Blood was
spreading out in a pool beneath her body. Some teenage boys ran
over. I thought they were going to help her, but they grabbed her
purse and ran off.
    I couldn't have helped her. There was too much blood. I
walked away. When I looked back, she was still lying there, her
arm at an odd angle, blood pooling around her body, all alone.
    I don't think he'll kill again. He killed the woman he loved.
Who else is he going to kill?
    Maybe I should have gone to the police, but I was afraid.
You read these novels, innocent guy at the scene of the crime, the
cops pin it on him because they can't find the real murderer, he
goes to the chair.
    I was afraid to go back.

Couldn't Say
By Christopher Wall

Ethan: thirties, emotionally shutdown

Dramatic

> *Liz has told her husband, Ethan, that their son appeared and talked to her after he died. Ethan, a professor and rigid intellectual, doesn't believe in souls or an afterlife. He hasn't been able to make sense of his son's death and has been trying hard not to think about it.*

ETHAN: So he came back and talked to you? That's — That's great. But why do you need me to believe it? I never went to church before he died. Or meditated. Or believed in souls, or the afterlife, or half the things I see in front of me. I doubt things for a living. And I've learned, as long as you have doubts about a thing, or the people you know, you'd be a fool to believe in them. Look. I used to try. Kept a picture of Mom on my dresser, growing up. Talked to her, looking for my sneakers in the morning. Before going to bed at night. But I never heard her or felt her presence. Where was she? Fluttering around in heaven? Hovering an inch away? Maybe she didn't exist at all, because there's no such thing as a soul. What do I know? I was nine years old. All I know is, it didn't matter if I put her picture on the dresser. Or in the dresser. Or talked. Or whispered. Or shouted. Or prayed. Or ignored her. Or cried and beat my fists against the wall. I didn't feel her presence. Ever. Anywhere. All I remember is lying in bed at night. Staring into the corner. Trying not to break.

Paralyzed July
By Kevin M. Lottes

Carl Warsaw: a paraplegic in his early thirties

Dramatic

> *Carl is an ex-soldier stuck in a wheelchair for the rest of his life. Because of this fact, his relationship with a longtime girlfriend is at stake. She feels as though she just can't go on living her life with a paraplegic. In reaction to her indifference toward him, Carl pops the big question. More than ever before, he is determined to keep her by his side.*

CARL: When I first laid eyes on you, that's when I had really lost all the nerves in my legs. No, I mean it. I've been walkin' funny ever since that night, so losin' my legs has been a happy accident in a way. Now I don't have to show everybody with every step I take just how hopelessly in love I am with you! So I suggest you let the word "yes" fall out between your lips, slide that damn ring on your finger, and tell me you'll be my wife. As much as you might hate me right now for confusin' the hell out of you when I came back from that dirty little war in a wheelchair, *you will love me.* It's just the way things go. It's the natural evolution of human beings — as long as they remember *to* love. You might hate me now, trying desperately to feel the way you felt the first time we met, but if you hang in there with that evolution, that's already laid out for you, and trust it, things do start to come back around eventually. Two people meet each other. They fall in love. They get crossed with each other. They break apart. They argue fuss and fight and then suddenly — right out of the blue — the ripples start to sway and you're right back to square one again. Just stick with me, July, and we'll make it! Whether we're walkin' or crawlin', we'll make it. I promise you.

A Death Defying Act
By Barbara Lindsay

Connor: thirties, is a man whose perspective on life has wholly changed with the news that he is mortally ill. His interest used to be in corporate wins; now he wants nothing more than all the closeness he can have with his beautiful, fearful wife. Connor himself has no fear at all.

Dramatic

Connor, who has cancer, has told his wife, Levaughn, that he wants to have a baby with her. She is hesitant, because of his illness.

CONNOR: Thanks to the well-intentioned Dr. Wilbur, I may be short a few million swimmers, but hey, I'm willing to give it my best shot. I mean, look around you, Vonny. With all due respect to everybody else, the gene pool needs us. Now, I know I never wanted to before. I have, I regret to say, been a perfect ass about some things. With the emphasis on perfect, of course. But don't you know half the reason I married you was I wanted to make a little Connor or Levaughn with you? First time I saw you, I thought, "Wow! Look at those chromosomes. Look at those nice wide hips. I give her a ten-hour labor, tops. Look at those breasts, just ripe for lactation. Look at that heart, that big, open heart which just pours all over a person until he feels safe in the world and ready for anything. Look at that face, which every baby should have the chance to wake up to in the morning." At the time, it probably looked as though all I was thinking was "Me want woman." But that's just guy talk for "I want to make a baby with you." I just didn't know how to say it until now. So think about it if you need to. I promise not to start without you.

AlligatoR
By Jeremy Menekseoglu

Ben: twenties to thirties, bag boy/ex-con

Seriocomic

> *Ben has fallen in love for the first time in his whole miser-*
> *able life. Nothing ever seems to work out for him. When*
> *Velvet tells him, within the hour of their first kiss, that she's*
> *moving away forever to a mental institution and she's leav-*
> *ing in the next five minutes, it is too much for his heart to*
> *take.*

BEN: Wait a sec — what the fuck's goin' on here? I really like you.
[Velvet: I like you.]
    Well, all right, thank you, bu' this don' make no sense. I felt
somethin' last night that I ain't ever felt in my life — Believe me,
if you was stayin' I wouldn' be tellin' you. It's this — uh, I mean,
I don' know much 'bout men'n women bu' I know that no weak
man ever got nobody, so I'm gonna feel real stupid sayin' this
jus' now OK? I ain't makin' no sense —
(Inhales. Pause.)
    OK . . . Last night, I'll admit, I was a little — you know —
really really drunk, an' that made me real real horny . . .
But . . . But . . . *(Stares.)*
    When you kissed me last night it wasn' jus' about fuckin'.
You know? It was . . . It was the most amazing thing that I ever
felt in my life. I was walkin' 'round on my tiptoes. I saw pictures
in my head of like beautiful forests and nighttime . . . With a
storm off in the distance. I could smell the perfume of the first
girl I ever kissed back in the sixth grade . . . After you left I was
sober. (Pause.)
    I cain't jus' let you — I mean, unless you didn' feel any of
that, an' I'm jus' some fuckin' psycho — you know? I cain't let
you go without some kind of fight.

Wall Street Hymn
By James Armstrong

Stan: a businessman in his thirties

Comic

> *Stan meets up with his colleague Mitchell at the American Museum of Natural History. When Mitchell tries to entice him with a possibly illegal stock deal that could make them both rich, Stan recounts how his new girlfriend is making him see that there's more to life than making money.*

STAN: You don't understand. There's this woman. . . . The way she walks. The way she speaks. The way she smells! It's unbelievable. It sorta turned me off at first, but I mean now I've gotten used to it, gotten to know her, even her sweat drives me crazy! When we met, for the first time, it was raining, pouring outside, and I stepped in this huge puddle, full of mud. I didn't care about the shoes. They were old shoes. But I'd just bought this new pair of Argyles. She promised to get me another pair. It was just a joke. I mean, she hardly knew me. Well, anyway, we met again. It was like a week later. Just by accident, we happened to bump into each other at the museum. *This* museum, actually. Right by the woolly mammoth. She reached into her purse, and she pulled out a brand new pair of Argyle socks. She'd been carrying them around ever since we'd met. All my life, there's always been one thing I wanted. And now, for the first time, it's not that important anymore. She is.

Flung
By Lisa Dillman

Jim: thirty-three

Seriocomic

In this monologue, Jim tells his wife, Meryl, why he's come back after having left her during a family reunion.

JIM: I got all the way to Newcastle. I was going ninety miles an hour — that little tin-can rental was shimmying all over the road. I kept thinking about you taking the train back like you said. Sitting there on one of those cruddy train seats. Looking out a smeary window. And striking up a conversation with some stranger. You know how people talk on trains. Tell each other things they would never tell *anyone* they were ever going to see again. I mean. I pictured you doing that. Telling some bank teller or teacher or social worker about me. About us. And that stranger — some nice, disappointed middle-aged woman, probably — was going to end up knowing me as just this sort of half-formed, clueless lug in a story she heard on a train . . . *I couldn't take that . . . I don't deserve that. (Beat.)*
   That story. The one you were telling about us on the train. It was all in the past tense. I had to come back . . . I had to talk to you . . . I miss that so much. Talking to you. I guess I just figured you'd always be my best friend. That's the part I really can't stand. Mer'. I want you to *like* me again.

7out
By Allan Staples

Francis: thirty, a sports talk radio host

Seriocomic

> *Francis is speaking to his ex-girlfriend who he hasn't seen in six months and is trying to convince her that she should move away with him.*

FRANCIS: I wanted to write you the most romantic thing you've ever heard so you'd come back to me. I wanted to knock you down with feeling. So I guess we can call this "Excerpts from a birthday card I didn't send you last month." *(Reciting from memory.)* If I was going to lose my sight, for some contrived romantic reason let's say, I was gonna lose my vision, you are the last thing that I'd want to see in this world. And if I was gonna lose my hearing, which might actually happen from wearing my headphones so loud all the time at work, the last thing I'd want to hear is you telling me that you loved me again, and fine, I could never hear a single thing again. Let those words be how I remember what sound was. Anyway, I hope you have a wonderful birthday and I do love you. Love, Francis. See, it's funny 'cause I used to hate when you'd say it, but now it's the last thing I'd want to hear. See, it's very ironic, very *Tales from the Crypt-ish*. A blind, deaf schmuck trying to host a radio show having sacrificed it all for the woman he loves. *(Beat.)* I know it's a long shot, but I love you and I think you still love me. And if you do, come with me. I've never been more sure about anything in my life.

A Greater Good
By Keith Huff

Morris Quimby: thirties

Seriocomic

> *Morris Quimby, an IRS auditor, has been sent to an island commune run by women to investigate them for nonpayment of taxes. He speaks to Melissa, a woman for whom in a previous scene he has expressed a dislike so severe, it can only stem from love. In this scene, the island setting and moonlight have softened him considerably.*

MORRIS: You think I'm awful, don't you? I *am* awful. I stink. I'm a stinking lousy bureaucrat who sold his spine for a government pension! Say, you're . . . beautiful, you know that? No, I mean it. First time I saw you. First thing I thought. That's why I poured on the bile. I find beauty terribly intimidating. Not now, no. Myopia and the moonlight have permitted you to bewitch me. I'm not married, if you're wondering. Not a homosexual, either. At the office, they all think that about me. I know they do, back-stabbing old hags. Civil servants are a sickening lot. I'm just no good at machismo, you know? Have you ever seen that film, Melissa? *Les Enfants du Paradis?* It's French. *L'amour . . . c'est très simple.* Love is very simple. I'm not sure about that. I'm not sure love is so very simple. Then there's beauty. Complicates matters to no end, beauty.

Horatio
By Chris Stezin

Bud: early to mid-thirties, a bartender for life and serial monogamist who let his one true love slip away.

Seriocomic

Bud's younger brother Thom comes to him for some advice on women.

BUD: So, you finally come to your big brother for advice and guidance. Hurts doesn't it? First time ever and what do you ask me about? Women? I guess you'd like me to cover cold fusion while we're at it. OK. Here we go. Look, first of all, never be honest with a woman, they don't like it. Oh, they might tell you that's what they want, but it's not what they want, and they don't know what they want. Trust me on this one. Honesty is a jumbo jet with bad hydraulics. It'll take you down quick. And that's about 50 percent of the sum total of my knowledge of the subject. But here's the other half. If, at some point, you happen to find yourself in a dimly lit restaurant with this beautiful woman you've told me about, and you look up to catch her staring at you, I mean, just drinking you in . . . well, you stare right back. And you do your best to take in every detail. The shape and color of her eyes, the curve of her lips, the way she laughs, the little freckles that run across the bridge of her nose. You store it all up, because a man's lucky if he has one moment like that in his whole life. And all this nonsense about, "I don't know if it can work out between us," well, goddamn it, man, just try, just do it. And if you know with a certainty that in two days or two months or two years this same woman will reach across the table into your chest, pull out your heart, and squeeze it dry right before your very eyes, well, you do it anyway. Do it anyway. Because it is a ride not to be missed, my friend. I highly recommend it . . . And that's everything I know about women.

The Big Vig
By Jason Furlani

Lenny: thirties, a mountain of a man with little-boy eyes. Lenny is an unemployed bricklayer, who married his high school sweetheart because they thought she was pregnant and wanted to "do the right thing."

Seriocomic

> *Lenny always does the "right thing." But when he reconnects with a childhood friend who, through no device of her own, reminds him of what it's like to feel alive he is left to contemplate doing the "right thing" versus happiness. Here Lenny struggles to convey his feelings to his "salt of the earth" father.*

LENNY: I know you don't understand how I could be in love with her. And I know you don't think I know who she is. But I gotta tell you Dad . . . I do. I really do. And what's more, she knows me. You know, I used ta bring her lilacs offa old man Peter's tree? I didn't remember that. *She* did. She remembered how I used ta like egg creams. And my bike with the yellow banana seat? You remember that? *She* did! She remembered my happiness. She remembered ME. An' I know I'm married, an' I know it ain't right ta' feel like this about another woman, an' I know I should just do like you say an' forget it all together. But every time I think about her, I get so much energy flowin' in me. Pulsin', pumpin' through my every vein . . . like I'm on fire. Like I'm the big sign down on top the G.E. plant. Burnin'. Lightin' up the Crosstown an' Erie Boulevard bright as day. And I can't ignore it. And it won't leave me alone. An', ta tell ya the God's honest truth . . . it feels GREAT! So I don't know. Maybe that ain't love. I don't know. Maybe it's just like some big alarm clock screamin' "WAKE UP, DUMMY! YOU'RE ALIVE!" I don't know. All's I do know is I don't wanna hit the snooze bar on this, wake up thirty years from now still starin' down the truth a the matter, which is . . . I ain't happy bein' me. And, so, no. No Dad. I don't expect you to *understand*, but, anyhow . . . that's what's goin' on.

Practicing Peace
By Kelly DuMar

Keith: a clinical psychologist who practices meditation, early thirties

Comic

> *The meditation room of Keith and Kiki's suburban home.*
> *Keith reacts to his wife's alarm over the squirrel who's rav-*
> *aging his bird feeder.*

KEITH: *(Rushing to window.)* What's the matter? Is he on top of the . . . ?
(Banging on window.)
   Hey! Get off my feeder, you bully! You hog! You big, fat pig! I'll get you yet, you trespasser!
(Opening window.)
   Hand me that candle! I'm going to teach him a lesson! I'm going to get rid of him for good!
(Aims candle out window.)
   Don't worry. I have perfect aim!
(Hurls candle.)
   Damn! Quick! Hand me another candle! I never miss twice!
(Hurling candle.)
   Take that you bullying son of a-Ha-ha! Gotcha! That's the last we'll see of Mr. Greedy Squirrel! *(Beat.)* Huh? *(Beat.)* No, I did not! I just grazed him. Just scared him, that's all. *(Looking out the window after the squirrel.)* It can't be. I just . . . he's all right! He's just trying to arouse your sympathy, so he can come back and rob us with impunity tomorrow! There he goes! Into the woods.
(A moment of silence. He closes the window.)
   He's gone! That's what we wanted, isn't it? I don't think he'll be back anytime soon. *(Beat. Thinking.)* Maybe I did get a little carried away. It's just that . . . I don't think it's fair for the birds to starve because he's a glutton! . . . Do you really think I broke his leg?

Olfactory Test
from *Occupational Hazards*
By Mark McCarthy

Geoffrey: thirties, normally mild-mannered

Seriocomic

> *Geoffrey is a civil engineer in his thirties who's been out of work for some time. His predicament has him a bit paranoid, and he finally snaps when he realizes he's come full circle.*

GEOFFREY: Mister Mumford, I'm sure some of the — Medford? I'm so sorry. I'm sure some of the other candidates for this job are — You know what? Never mind. It doesn't matter. I sense it already. Since I got fi — Since I changed career paths, I have been to fifty-seven interviews, and they inevitably sort of grind down to this one moment where, no matter how desperately the guy tries to hide it, or the woman for that matter; plenty of women, where no matter how desperately they try to hide it; the decision has been made. Sometimes I think I can smell it. Do you fart when you do it? Or sweat or something? 'Cause I can smell it.

Don't talk. I'm talking.

Oh, my God. OH. MY. GOD. It's you. You were my very first interview. There is no escape. It's like in the movies. "We passed this place once before."

Please be quiet. I have to think this through.

If you're the same guy that first rejected me; and I think the olfactory test has come back positive on that one, Doctor Bob; that means that I've worked my way through every firm in my field in this city.

Shut up. *(Pause.)* I SAID SHUT UP!

Why does everyone hate me? I'm an OK guy. Not great, but OK. Well, all right maybe a little below average on many scales, but damn it! There are plenty of guys out there who are just as pathetic as me. I demand to know. What is it mister?

FOR THE LOVE OF GOD TELL ME WHAT MY PROBLEM IS!

Open Spaces
By Susan Kim

Ben: early thirties, neurotic

Comic

> *Highly neurotic Ben, early thirties, impulsively and unwisely takes off on a cross-country trip with his friend Sylvia. Their car breaks down and they find themselves in the middle of nowhere.*

BEN: It's this feeling I have. This funny, jangling feeling I've had ever since we got in the car. Because what started as a funny jangling feeling turned into a . . . queasy sinking feeling. Which wasn't so bad, but now it's turned into something else. A choking, gripping, nausea feeling. My throat is constricted, I can barely unclench my jaw. And I think the problem here isn't execution, it's high concept. Tearing up and down dirt roads on a whim, going wherever our hearts desire — it doesn't work, Sylvia. Which would not only explain why it took us three hours to get out of the Bronx, but also why after three days of driving, this is where we end up. A dead end in the middle of nowhere. I mean, just look at it. *(They do.)*

Do you know what my worst dream is? It's being trapped somewhere ugly, somewhere horrible — somewhere very much like this, in fact — and yet somehow not really knowing where I am exactly and how I got there. Look around. Smell it. Touch it. This is it. This is my nightmare.

"Will You Please Shut Up?"
By Dan O'Brien

Tom: twenties to early thirties

Comic

> *Tom is apologizing for losing his temper at Sylvia. Rather than admit their relationship is experiencing some significant "growing pains," he blames it on a psychosomatic rash; he wants to know where he got it from.*

TOM: I'm sorry, Syl.
It's my fault.
There's no excuse for how I've been acting. I think it's these hives I've got. Have I mentioned my hives? At first I thought it was some early symptom of West Nile encephalitis, then I thought maybe, who knows, "the clap." — I can't believe I'm telling you this after so long keeping it to myself . . . — Do people still get "the clap" anymore? I don't really know. And if I must sign my name as "Signore Gonorrhea," where did I get it from? From who? You? We're monogamous, right? I mean, we're not like the bonobo monkeys, are we? the most promiscuous animals in the animal kingdom who go so far in their friendliness as to give complete strangers genitals-kisses in response to the slightest hint of affection — no, we're a loving, young, *"human"* couple. But maybe you had the clap before we met . . . and you didn't know? Is it possible? Maybe that ex-boyfriend of yours, that one in the devil-rock band, that really rancid hair-band from St. Paul, maybe he got it off one of his groupies and passed it off to you? Huh? Do you think it's possible? It's possible, right? Which gets me thinking some pretty morbid thoughts, really morbid things I'm embarrassed even to admit about the meaning of irony and wouldn't it be ironic if some teenage groupie in Minnesota gave me the clap? or worse, you know, through the matrix of your ex-boyfriend, and I, who have not had sex with more than three people in my entire adult human lifetime die of The Clap. *(Beat.)*
But it also got me thinking nice thoughts.

Nice, profound thoughts. Like:

If people are capable of being connected to all these other people through webs of diseases or viruses or the Internet, then isn't it possible, just possible, that we're all connected by *good* things too, say the finer points, say "love"?

The Usual
By Barbara Lindsay

Clark: thirties, is a Master of the Universe–type businessman, driven, successful, wears the right clothes, drives the right car, knows the right people. And he has just learned that none of that makes the slightest difference.

Seriocomic

Clark is a successful businessman having lunch at his regular bistro. This afternoon he is demanding special treatment from his waitress, Staci.

CLARK: Well now, yes, I know that, I know you don't serve baked potatoes until five, but Staci, I'd like you to make an exception today, because, to tell you the truth, I really want that baked potato. I think I want it just about as much as I have ever wanted anything in my entire life. I've been thinking about it all the way from the . . . All the way here. Would you do that? Would you make an exception for me today, for no other reason than because you know it would mean a lot to me? I mean, do you have any idea how long it's been since I've had a baked potato with butter? Do you have any idea how long it's been since I did anything for just the pleasure of it? I've been vegetarian for eight years. No coffee, no booze, no drugs, no processed foods, no refined sugar or flour, low fat, high fiber, meditation, yoga, Audubon Society, recycling. I run three miles a day, I'm always on time, I've never shoplifted, never, *never* bounced a check. I don't hurt anybody. I found a cricket in my bedroom last week, but I didn't kill it. I put it outside, I let it live. *I let the cricket live.* Do you see what I'm saying? I *deserve* a baked potato. I've tried to do the right thing every day of my goddamned *life,* and I can't get a baked potato, I can't get respect, I can't get a little decent human kindness in a restaurant I have frequented for years? You won't do this *one little thing* for me? I WANT THAT BAKED POTATO! I NEED THAT BAKED POTATO! Wait, wait. Please. I'm . . . I'm . . . There's something growing in the back . . . at the base of my . . . I'm . . . I've just come from the hospital.

The Cup
By Barbara Lhota and Janet B. Milstein

Eric Silver: thirties, an appraiser for Sotheby's in New York

Comic

> *Rosie has taken her precious family treasure to the* Antiques
> Assembly, *a TV show that travels from town to town bring-*
> *ing several famous appraisers to assess the quality of the*
> *items local folks bring to the event. Rosie finally arrives at*
> *the front of the line. She will be speaking with the famous,*
> *English-born Eric Silver who works at Sotheby's in New*
> *York. Eric, sick of his job, is in a rush to weed through the*
> *hordes of people with worthless and uninteresting items.*

ERIC: How unfortunate. That it dented the cup of course. But the
problem, my dear lady, is that these dents and scratches could be
caused by someone dropping it in the mud several times, throwing it against someone's face, slamming a sledgehammer over it's
base and running it over with a bus several times. One does not
know that it has any connection to any battle, and particularly
the Battle of Bunker Hill. Additionally, it does not appear to be
that old. It *could* be because, in fact, tin is old, though worth
almost nothing. But after careful examination for signatures,
there is nothing to date it back to the 1700s or any battle at all.
And while it may be from some battle with no proof, in the eyes
of dealers, it is not. It is quite simply, a cup, with several
unsightly dents and a rather brownish encrust — ment. And as
for whether Vincent Van Gogh drank out of it? Perhaps this now
explains why he went mad.

Ticked Off in Toledo
By Justin Warner

Ted: thirties

Comic

> *Ted has paid a surprise visit on Nancy, a famous advice columnist. They have never met before, but Ted has a bone to pick with her. At the top of the play, she is bound and gagged as Ted unleashes his frustration.*

TED: I guess you're wondering why I've put you in this position. *(Nancy nods.)*
Good. It's flattering to be the recipient of your undivided attention. I know you've got a lot of letters to answer, don't you, Nancy?
(He waits for an answer, which obviously she can't provide.)
Nancy, do you know who I am?
(Nancy shakes her head "no.")
Of course not. Allow me to refresh your memory.
(Reciting from memory.)
"Dear Nancy: My wife and I have been happily married for nine years. I have only one complaint. *(Making quotation marks with his fingers, to indicate pseudonym)* 'Gladys' constantly leaves me notes telling me what to do. 'Don't forget to pick up the dry cleaning.' 'The new place mats go fuzzy side down.' 'If you open the pickles, put the rest back in the fridge!' *(Pause. Sighs.)* Nancy, I appreciate a helpful reminder as much as the next guy, but my wife is treating me like a four-year-old. Should I call this matter to her attention? Sincerely, Ticked Off in Toledo."
Remember that?
(Nancy nods.)
Good.
(He takes out a newspaper clipping.)
Your reply, four months later:
"Dear Ticked: By all means, tell 'Gladys' the notes are driving you bonkers. After nine years of wedded bliss, she should be able to handle the feedback."

(Pregnant pause.)

Well, she LEFT me! What do you think of THAT?

(Nancy shrugs, at a loss.)

I guess your half-baked advice isn't all it's cracked up to be, huh? I guess you're not so smart after all! Well, now I've got you where I want you, Nancy, and I have one thing to ask you!

Do you think she'll take me back?

In the Centerfold
By Jonathan Bernstein

Governor Franklin Kennedy Adams: thirty-nine, a poster boy/man
  for the Party

Comic

> *The governor is romancing a young staffer named Samantha*
> *late at night in the mansion and is horrified as they watch a*
> *stand-up comic lampoon him on a television talk-show.*

GOVERNOR FRANKLIN KENNEDY ADAMS: I can't believe that. I cannot
believ — who does he think he is? Can you? — why would
he — why would he say — and on television? — because I'm
basically — I'm trying here, is all. I am just trying here, Saman-
tha, every day — every hour of every — there's no need for that,
that, for that kind of humor — that sick kind of easy sort of
humor, and on national television? — because you should know
that being governor of this state is very hard work, and there is
a lot of work to do, and I am trying to get it all done, I really
am. Yet people mock.

God, that makes me feel so — this job is extremely diffi —
people don't know, Sam — no one knows. The other *governors,*
maybe they know, fine, but no one else, no one else, because not
everyone can be — and I can do more, OK, yes, there's more to
do, but I am giving it everything, every d — there is something
about this job that makes people think they can just take advan-
ta — there are people in receiving lines who try to crack my fingers when they shake my hand. Imagine? Strangers — people I
don't even personally know — are trying to, what?, break my
hand, so they can tell their friends that they crushed the governor's knuckles or something. It's like a game with them, like a,
like a dirty knuckle game. A knuckle-crushing-crush-the-
governor's-knuckles knuckle game or something, this world, I
am telling you, is so negative. There is such cynicism.

God I hope I don't get reelected. I have a whole list of other
things I want to do with my life that is the best argument for
term limits you ever heard . . . Do you have to go?

Stopgap
By Mary Portser

Ray: thirties, a dissatisfied L.A. actor now working in sales

Comic

> *Ray's been having an affair with Evie, a new salesperson,*
> *who he's been advising. Suddenly Evie out-bests him. Ray*
> *can't take it and accuses her of cheating. Now she's giving*
> *him the shoulder. Here he's trying to justify his behavior and*
> *win her back.*

RAY: I didn't want to report you, Evie. But you were cheating. Believe me, it hurt me worse than you. Don't shut me out, baby. Please. I need you. You know the kind of year I've been having. I was supposed to be a star by now. Everyone who's on my team has let me down. Lana clogs her arteries and gives herself a heart attack. So the agency replaces her with Jerry of the subhuman intelligence. Jerry, who I wined and dined at every vegetarian restaurant in Los Angeles. You know I did that. Analyzing my career trajectory. The roles I would play, the build. He hung on my every word. Suddenly the auditions stop. I'm the forgotten man. So I call the office — ready to do a number on Jerry's head. And the secretary says to me: "Ray, he's dead. You're not getting any auditions because Jerry's dead. He committed suicide." The bastard. So all I really have in my life — that I'm good at — is this lousy sales job. And when I see you trying to take it away from me — to best me, to undermine me. I feel like I want to kill you and then myself. Shhh. Don't say anything. I love you even though you're poison to me. You seep through my blood like a deadly virus. You're the best thing that ever happened to me, baby.

Burning Down the House
By Barbara Lhota and Janet B. Milstein

Tony: thirties, Marissa's husband

Dramatic

> *Marissa's quirky hypochondria and obsessive-compulsive behavior have become worse since having their baby a year ago. Lately, her behavior has become less quirky and more harmful to their relationship. In this speech, Tony feels compelled to ask her to seek help.*

TONY: That's not the point anymore. The point now is that you *have* to check it. And it's not for anyone's welfare exactly. And you don't have to just check the stove. You check the sink in the bathroom to make sure the faucet isn't on. And that light switch. I know you do. I've seen you when you think I'm not watching. Then you check the shower. And then you walk over to the candles, that haven't been lit for days, to make sure they're put out. There are all kinds of mistakes and accidents out there, Marissa. There're undetected gas leaks and carbon dioxide poisons and knives left in wrong places. There are dangerous chemicals left near open flames. Faulty wiring that you would have discovered had you had the electrician come in that one more time. The whole house is a horror if you let it be. And it's not just about the house anymore. Last week do you know how many tests you asked to have run on Timmy? *(Beat.)* Sometimes it doesn't matter how careful you are. Things just happen. I think I need you to get help, Marissa.

Nirvana
By Barbara Lindsay

Eric: thirties, is a blue-collar man, charming, sexy, physically strong, but very insecure. He wants to be a good man, but he can't help following his impulses and drives.

Dramatic

> *Eric has come to his ex-wife Glynnis's apartment to collect a wedding present she has for him and his fiancée Darleen. Glynnis and Eric end up making love. It is now half an hour later.*

ERIC: I guess I better get going. I don't know what to say except — wow. I mean, I'm really glad that, you know, that there are still some good feelings there. Sort of a nice little salute at the end before we go our separate ways. So I guess I'd better go now. Glynnis? Are you all right? *(Beat.)* OK, so I'm on my way. I'll see you or talk to you or whatever. Thanks for the juicer. *(Beat.)* Actually, I probably don't need to say this, but I'd like to keep this pretty much between us. I mean, I wouldn't want Darleen to think, you know, anything. She wouldn't understand the situation and it would hurt her feelings pretty bad. I mean, I know you wouldn't, but I just want to be sure we're clear. I know I've caused you a lot of hurt and I just don't want to pass any of that on to Darleen. So what do you say? Can we let this be a private thing? All right, baby? *(Beat.)* What's with the silent treatment? Are you going to sit there or do I have your word that you are not going to pass the news along to Darleen? *(Beat.)* Yeah, OK, I get it. It's the needling thing again. You need to dance around a while, watch him squirm, maybe he'll sweat a little, right? You want me nervous? I'm nervous. You want the hands to shake? They're shaking. All right? The ulcer is acting up and I'm on the way to begging. Now cut the crap and promise me on your life that this is private. *(Beat.)* You bitch! You bitch! You bitch! You bitch! You bitch! If you speak to her, I'll tear your face off. Why do you want to do that? When is it enough? When is it enough?

4 MURDERS by Brett Neveu. ©2004 by Brett Neveu. Reprinted by permission of the author. All inquiries should be directed to John Buzzetti, The Gersh Agency, 41 Madison Avenue, 33rd Floor, New York, NY 10010; (212) 634-8126; jbuzzetti@gershny.com

7OUT by Allan Staples. ©2001 by Allan Staples. Reprinted by permission of the author. All inquiries should be addressed to Allan_c_stapls@hotmail.com

THE ALIEN HYPOTHESIS by William Borden. ©1994 by William Borden. Reprinted by permission of the author. All inquiries should be addressed c/o Rachel Purcell, 7996 S. FM 548, Royse City, TX 75189; borden@ev1.net

ALLIGATOR by Jeremy Menekseoglu. ©1998 by Jeremy Menekseoglu. Reprinted by permission of the author. All inquiries should be addressed to No4thwall@gmail.com; www.dreamtheatrecompany.com

THE ART OF THE FORECAST by Dennis Schebetta. ©2004 by Dennis Schebetta. Reprinted by permission of the author. All inquiries should be addressed to denschebetta@hotmail.com

AUNT RAINI by Tom Smith. ©2003 by Tom Smith. Reprinted by permission of the author. All inquiries should be addressed to kirbysr@hotmail.com

A BAD WEEK FOR THERAPY by Barbara Lhota and Janet B. Milstein. ©2003 by Barbara Lhota and Janet B. Milstein. Reprinted by permission of the authors. Originally published in *Forensics Series Volume 1, Duo Practice and Competition: 35 8-10 Minute Original Comedic Plays*. All inquiries should be directed to Barbara Lhota at blhota@aol.com and to Janet B. Milstein at act4you@msn.com, monologues@msn.com

BIG NIGHT by N. M. Brewka. ©2004 by N. M. Brewka. Reprinted by permission of the author. All inquiries should be addressed to clarx@shore.net

THE BIG VIG by Jason Furlani. ©2004 by Jason Furlani. Reprinted by permission of the author. For future rights/script inquiries, please contact: Josselyne Herman-Saccio, Josselyne Herman & Associates, 345 East 56th St., Suite 3B, New York, NY 10022; E-mail: dreamreve@aol.com

BILLY AND DAGO by Charles Evered. ©1988 by Charles Evered. Reprinted by permission of the author. All inquiries should be addressed to CBEvered@aol.com

BLACK NOW BLUE by Adam Simon. ©2001 by Adam Simon. Reprinted by permission of the author. All inquiries should be addressed to adamsimon@gmail.com

BRIDEWELL by Charles Evered. ©2001 by Charles Evered. Reprinted by permission of the author. All inquiries should be addressed to CBEvered@aol.com

BURNING DOWN THE HOUSE by Barbara Lhota and Janet B. Milstein. ©2003 by Barbara Lhota and Janet B. Milstein. Reprinted by permission of the authors. Originally published in *Forensics Series Volume 2, Duo Practice and Performance: 35 8-10 Minute Original Dramatic Plays*. All inquiries should be directed to Barbara Lhota at blhota@aol.com and to Janet B. Milstein at act4you@msn.com, monologues@msn.com

CASTLES ON THE COAST OF NORTH CAROLINA by John Michael Manship. ©2003 by John Michael Manship. Reprinted by permission of the author. All inquiries should be addressed to 471 Medford St., Somerville, MA 02145; E-mail: mike@southcitytheatre.org

THE COST OF MATHEMATICS by L. Pontius. ©2005 by L. Pontius. Reprinted by permission of the author. All inquiries should be addressed to muijo@juno.com

COULDN'T SAY by Christopher Wall. ©2001 by Christopher Wall. Reprinted by permission of the author. All inquiries should be addressed to www.christopherwall.org

THE COWBOY WHO USED A DALLY ROPE by Dylan Guy. ©2003 by Dylan Guy. Reprinted by permission of the author. All inquiries should be addressed to 233 E. 21st. St. #21, New York, NY 10010; E-mail: Dylan_Guy1@yahoo.com

THE CUP by Barbara Lhota and Janet B. Milstein. ©2003 by Barbara Lhota and Janet B. Mil-

Dramatic Publishing Company, 311 Washington Street, Woodstock, IL 60098. Barbara Lindsay's E-mail: lindsaybarb@comcast.net
HAY by Cynthia Franks. ©2005 by Cynthia Franks. Reprinted by permission of the author. All inquiries should be addressed to CynFrank@aol.com
THE HOPE CAMPAIGN by Erica Rosbe. ©2004 by Erica Rosbe. Reprinted by permission of the author. All inquiries should be addressed to Enr205@nyu.edu
HORATIO by Chris Stezin. ©2003 by Chris Stezin. Reprinted by permission of the author. All inquiries should be addressed to cstezin@yahoo.com
HOW TO DRAW MYSTICAL CREATURES by Ellen Margolis. ©2004 by Ellen Margolis. Reprinted by permission of the author. All inquiries should be addressed to emdm154@hotmail.com
HURRICANE IRIS by Justin Warner. ©2002 by Justin Warner. Reprinted by permission of the author. All inquiries should be addressed to jwarner@alum.haverford.edu; Web site: www.justinwarner.net
I-2195 by Barbara Lindsay. ©2003 by Barbara Lindsay. Reprinted by permission of the author. All inquiries should be addressed to Barbara Lindsay at lindsaybarb@comcast.net
IF ONLY by Barbara Lhota and Janet B. Milstein. ©2003 by Barbara Lhota and Janet B. Milstein. Reprinted by permission of the authors. Originally published in *Forensics Series Volume 2, Duo Practice and Performance: 35 8-10 Minute Original Dramatic Plays*. All inquiries should be directed to Barbara Lhota at blhota@aol.com and to Janet B. Milstein at act4you@msn.com, monologues@msn.com
IF THIS ISN'T LOVE by Jonathan Bernstein. ©2004 by Jonathan Bernstein. Reprinted by permission of the author. All inquiries should be addressed to E-mail: jonnymize@earthlink.net
IN THE CENTERFOLD by Jonathan Bernstein. ©2003 by Jonathan Bernstein. Reprinted by permission of the author. All inquiries should be addressed to E-mail: jonnymize@earthlink.net
IN THE COOP by Andrea Goyan. ©1991 by Andrea Goyan. Reprinted by permission of the author. All inquiries should be addressed to mrgmaximus@hotmail.com
INTO THE WIND by Adrienne Perry. ©2003 by Adrienne Perry. Reprinted by permission of the author. All inquiries should be addressed tocubrienne_rottweilers@hotmail.com
JOHNNY FLIP'S FATE by Chris Howlett. ©2003 by Chris Howlett. Reprinted by permission of the author. All inquiries should be addressed to howlettchris@hotmail.com
LAST LOVE by Peter Papadopoulos. ©2005 by Peter Papadopoulos. Reprinted by permission of the author. All inquiries should be addressed to Peter@PeterPop.com; Web site: www.peterpop.com
THE LAST STAND OF THE COMANCHE RIDER by Elise Forier. ©1999 by Elise Forier. Reprinted by permission of the author. All inquiries should be addressed to foriere1590@cwu.edu
LET A HUNDRED FLOWERS BLOOM by David Zellnik. ©2000 by David Zellnik. Reprinted by permission of the author. All inquiries should be addressed to Zellnik@hotmail.com or (212) 388-7903 (Answering Service)
THE LINE SHACK by Kevin M. Lottes. ©2004 by Kevin M. Lottes. Reprinted by permission of the author. All inquiries should be addressed to Kevin M. Lottes, *barehanded books,* P.O. Box 508, Westerville, OH 43086; 614-783-8702; kevin@barehandedbooks.com; www.barehandedbooks.com
MANAGEMENT ORIENTATION by Adam Simon. ©2004 by Adam Simon. Reprinted by permission of the author. All inquiries should be addressed to adamsimon@gmail.com
MARVEL by Joshua Scher. ©2004 by Joshua Scher. Reprinted by permission of the author. All inquiries should be addressed to mailjosh@screwyscrawler.com
MEN-OH-PAUSE by Lauren D. Yee. ©2004 by Lauren D. Yee. Reprinted by permission of the author. All inquiries should be addressed to laurendyee@hotmail.com
THE MOMENT OF TRUTH from *CRAZYOLOGY* by Frank Higgins. ©2005 by Frank Higgins.

ST. COLM'S INCH by Robert Koon. ©1997 by Robert Koon. Reprinted by permission of the author. All inquiries should be addressed c/o Chicago Dramatists, 1105 W. Chicago Avenue, Chicago, IL 60622. www.chicagodramatists.org

STOPGAP by Mary Portser. ©2004 by Mary Portser. Reprinted by permission of the author. All inquiries should be addressed to Mary Portser, 918-1/2 Palms Blvd., Venice, CA 90291.

STRANGERS IN LAMAZE by Mark W. Cornell. ©1997 by Mark W. Cornell. Reprinted by permission of the author. All inquiries should be addressed to markcornell53@yahoo.com

STUCK OUTSIDE OF DAYTON WITH THE BOB DYLAN BLUES AGAIN by Dennis Schebetta. ©2004 by Dennis Schebetta. Reprinted by permission of the author. All inquiries should be addressed to denschebetta@hotmail.com

SYSTEM ETERNAL by Chance D. Muehleck. ©2003 by Chance D. Muehleck. Reprinted by permission of the author. All inquiries should be addressed to cmuehleck@yahoo.com

TAPSTER by N. M. Brewka. ©2004 by N. M. Brewka. Reprinted by permission of the author. All inquiries should be addressed to clarx@shore.net

TEN ACROBATS IN AN AMAZING LEAP OF FAITH by Yussef El Guindi. ©2003 by Yussef El Guindi. Reprinted by permission of the author. All inquiries should be addressed to yelg@mindspring.com

THE TESTIMONY OF GARY ALAN RICHARDS by Rohn Jay Miller. ©2004 by Rohn Jay Miller. Reprinted by permission of the author. All inquiries should be addressed to Rohn Jay Miller, 1801 Dupont Avenue South, Minneapolis, MN 55403; rohn@millerusa.com

TICKED OFF IN TOLEDO by Justin Warner. ©1999 by Justin Warner. Reprinted by permission of the author. All inquiries should be addressed to jwarner@alum.haverford.edu; www.justinwarner.net

TODD AND GUY GO CAMPING by Barbara Lindsay. ©1995 by Barbara Lindsay. Reprinted by permission of the author. All inquiries should be addressed to Barbara Lindsay at lindsaybarb@comcast.net

TRACES by Charles Evered. ©1990 by Charles Evered. Reprinted by permission of the author. All inquiries should be addressed to CBEvered@aol.com

UNTOLD CRIMES OF INSOMNIACS by Janet Allard. ©2004 by Janice Allard. Reprinted by permission of the author. Commissioned by the Guthrie Theater, Joe Dowling, Artistic Director. All inquiries should be addressed to janet.allard@aya.yale.edu

THE USUAL by Barbara Lindsay. ©1997 by Barbara Lindsay. Reprinted by permission of the author. All inquiries should be addressed to Barbara Lindsay at lindsaybarb@comcast.net

WALL STREET HYMN by James Armstrong. ©2005 by James Armstrong. Reprinted by permission of the author. All inquiries should be addressed to jstanleydickens@aol.com; 357 W. 45th Street, Apt. 1RE, New York, NY 10036.

THE WET SCIENCE by Benjamin Sahl. ©2005 by Ben Sahl. Reprinted by permission of the author. All inquiries should be addressed to Sahl2005@lawnet.ucla.edu

WHAT HE CAN'T TELL YOU by Mark Loewenstern. ©2005 by Mark Loewenstern. Reprinted by permission of the author. All inquiries should be directed through Samuel French, Inc., 45 West 25th Street, New York, NY 10010.

WHATEVER HAPPENED TO GODOT? by Jonathan Dorf. ©2004 by Jonathan Dorf. Reprinted by permission of Brooklyn Publishers, 1841 Cord Street, Odessa, TX 79762. All inquiries should be addressed to Jonathan Dorf. E-mail address: jon@jondorf.com. Web site: www.jondorf.com.

WHISPERS IN THE WIND by Melissa Gawlowski. ©2004 by Melissa Gawlowski. Reprinted by permission of the author. All inquiries should be addressed to mgawlowski@hotmail.com

"WILL YOU PLEASE SHUT UP?" by Dan O'Brien. ©2005 by Dan O'Brien. All rights reserved. Reprinted by permission of Playscripts, Inc. To purchase acting editions of this play, or to obtain stock and amateur performance rights, you must contact: Playscripts, Inc. Web site: http://www.playscripts.com; E-mail: info@playscripts.com. Phone: 1-866-NEW-PLAY (639-7529)